On
Becoming
A
Grandparent

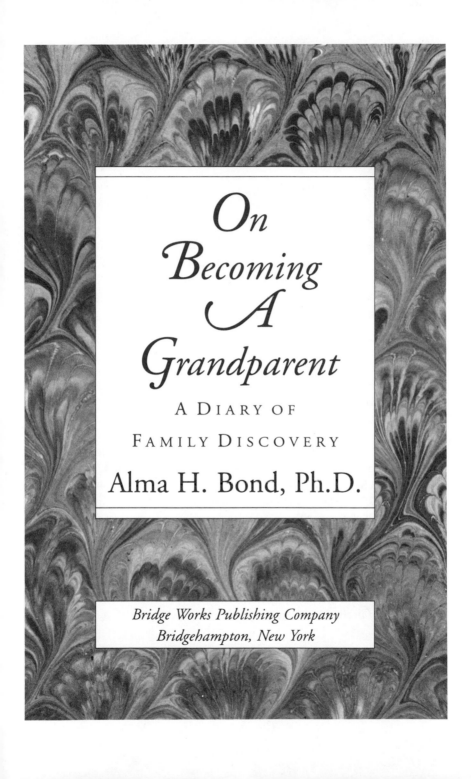

On Becoming A Grandparent

A DIARY OF FAMILY DISCOVERY

Alma H. Bond, Ph.D.

Bridge Works Publishing Company
Bridgehampton, New York

Library of Congress Cataloging-in-Publication Data

Bond, Alma Halbert.
    On becoming a grandparent : a diary of family discovery / Alma H. Bond.—1st ed.
      p.   cm.
    ISBN 1-882593-08-1 (hard cover, acid-free paper)
    1. Grandparents—United States—Family relationships. 2. Grandparenting—United States. 3. Grandparent and child—United States. I. Title.
  HQ759.9.B66   1994
  306.874′5—dc20   94-9051
                                                  CIP

10 9 8 7 6 5 4 3 2 1

Book and jacket design by Edith Allard
Printed in the United States of America

To my grandchildren,
Rachel, Alex, Mia, and Matthew.

Contents

FOREWORD

I wrote this book as a psychoanalyst and human being, to instruct and entertain those who, like me, imagined that a grandchild would fully close the family circle, disturbing very little the dynamics of coexistence. I seldom have been more wrong. Any family conflicts not fully resolved reappear with a new birth, affecting the family as totally as a baleful disease. No secret corner, no hiding place remains untouched by the presence of the new family member. I hope my diary and the analysis of my dream worlds and those of others will be useful and reassure those who have also felt guilt and anguish about an experience that, to the casual observer, should be a completely blessed event.

I wish to express gratitude to my children, Janet, Jonathan, and Zane, and their respective spouses, Sam, Wendy, and Judy, for their generosity in allowing me to use material from their lives. I realize that analyzing one's own family is foolhardy, perhaps dangerous, and that my authority, Sigmund Freud, would probably not approve. However, I am taking the chance.

Alma Halbert Bond
January 1994

ACKNOWLEDGMENTS

I am indebted to my publishers, Barbara and Warren Phillips, for believing in my book from their first reading. I particularly want to thank Barbara, who, along with Peg Lower, edited the manuscript. I also wish to thank my friends Leslie Hermann, Martha Van Noppen, Lois Barrowcliff, and members of the Key West Writers' Group, for their valuable critiques of early versions of the manuscript, as well as Anne Burstein's 1990 class in novel writing at Barnard College.

On
Becoming
A
Grandparent

Dreams and Reality

February 23, 1987

AT 6:30 THIS MORNING, I was riding my exercycle when the phone rang. Usually I don't hear the phone when I'm on the machine, but today I did. It was my daughter Janet calling from Florida. I felt a faint apprehension.

"Guess what, Mommy, I'm pregnant," she sang out. My heart missed a beat. I expressed the usual happiness and good wishes and hung up to think about the new development.

In the first place, I feel too old to be a grandmother for the first time. When she was angry with my niece Susan, her first grandchild, my mother would say, "Fifty years I've waited for this?" I'd waited a lot longer—64 years, to be exact. I've been ready to be a grandmother for years, but my children have been taking their time with their lives.

I'm not pleased with my first reactions. I should be as happy as Janet, delighted that there will be new life to contribute to my growth as an individual, but I'm not. One tends to think of children as contributing to one's growth, but I'm now imagining that mine have held up my development. I feel alone, like an undiscovered planet circling remotely in space. Something must be wrong with me.

My reactions are so different from those of my own mother. I was first pregnant in 1950 in Chicago, when my husband Rudy was an actor on the road with Melvyn Douglas in *Two Blind Mice.* After the Saturday night show, we drove our little two-seater Hudson all night to Philadelphia, where my parents lived, to surprise them with the news. My parents were waiting for us at the door of their row house. Like the dried autumn leaves rustling on their sidewalk, life changed color for all of us that day; something deep shifted the former tempo of our relationship into a slower, more encapsulated moment. We all ended up crying together. And years later, when my twins were born and I presented the two little babies to my mother with their Hebrew names, Meyer and Frima Laya in honor of her parents, she said, "I've got my mother and father back." Why do I not have those sentiments with Janet's news?

My children have always been very different from each other. We used to say that our family consisted of all chiefs and no Indians. That didn't change as the children became adults.

My daughter Janet has olive skin and blue eyes, which tend to make her look exotic. But she is an all-American girl, with a passionate interest in running, swimming, and other health-related pastimes, who specializes in exercise physiology and nutrition. She and her husband, Sam, live in Florida, far from me in New York. They say they live there so they can swim and run outdoors all year round. But when I learned of the baby, I wondered if that was the whole story, if they needed to live far from their parents, all in the north. Suddenly I saw that my daughter was gaining emotional distance from me by putting miles between us. Sam, whose superb self-confidence has allowed him to hold his own among a number of my psychoanalytic friends, all of whom have much more formal education than he, may even have been the instigator of this distance. I wonder if he will even permit me to hold his baby.

Janet's twin, Jonathan, is the president of Kirschenbaum and Bond Advertising Agency. Creative and with a good business sense, he and Wendy, his pretty wife, are model cosmopolites, complete with a BMW. He wears Hermès ties, she Gucci scarves. They live at a fashionable address in New York City, uncannily forecasting trends in clothing, art, and lifestyles.

Zane, my oldest child, is tall, handsome, and somewhat overweight. Unlike Jon, he couldn't care less about prevailing trends. Friends refer to my sons as "the hippie and the yuppie." Zane was a victim of the sixties: his experimentation with LSD set off a chemical imbalance, which led to a bipolar illness that threatened his sanity for years. He fought desperately to regain his health. He and his wife, Judy, will not have children but will concentrate instead on his mental health and the success of their marriage. Judy, who is from the Philippines, is ideal for

Zane; she is accepting and loving, without pressuring him for material success.

My children are close to me as well as happily married, but they don't seem very interested in each other. We called the twins Jonathan and Janet, the "Bond Law of Fair Distribution of Progeny," two babies in 1957 to make up for a miscarriage I had had several years earlier. Yet today, I think they wouldn't mind if they never saw each other again. I would like my children to feel close to each other, particularly after I am gone. Perhaps there is jealousy among them still, and I can't help but feel it is my fault. I remember reading once that if siblings fight too much, there is too much parenting. Step back and fade into the woodwork, the author advised. I'm afraid I've never been one to fade into the woodwork. Or perhaps it's simply that mothers are programmed to carry only one fetus at a time, and twins, like the pearl in the oyster, are a beautiful irritant to their host.

♣

March 10

SUDDENLY, WE HAVE ALL BEGUN TO DREAM. As a Freudian psychoanalyst, dreams have always been important to me. I believe they are the most important repository of the unconscious, the blueprint for conflict and hidden emotions.

According to Freud, dreams are the "royal road to the unconscious." Through the study of dreams, Freud entered into the secret life of his patients as no one had before. More than any teacher, Freud's *Interpretation of*

Dreams has made me the person I am today. I interpret my own and others' dreams with excitement as well as a professional interest that has almost always proved valid. I also find dreams of primary importance in treating my patients. Dreams help them get in touch with the essence of their being. Then I teach them to analyze their own dreams and become independent of me.

I have kept a record of my dreams from the time I was 21 years old, long before I became a professional analyst. Whenever I am in a crisis or don't understand what is going on in my life, I turn to dreams for help. More often than not, the answers are inbedded in them.

Now, Janet writes of a dream that her baby is born and I come to visit. I tell her what to do to take care of the child. "Mommy," she exclaims, "this is *my* baby and *I'm* the one in charge, not you!" It is obvious that having her own child will help her become more her own person. It is a healthy development, and the dream points out her essential strength and good health. Why, then, do I still feel sad?

♣

April 1

MY GRANDCHILD'S PERVASIVE new influence in my life became clear to me last night in a dream of my own: Janet and I are visiting a strange city and are ready to go home. In the cab, I remember I have left my white running suit in a brown paper bag in the lobby of the hotel. I must reclaim the suit before we can go home. The gruff cabby says, "You can have five minutes." In the hotel I find Janet

Dreams and Reality

5

and Sam watching a show with what I think is my package. It isn't. I reach for it and a large clothesline full of clean laundry falls down, almost to the ground. As I leave empty-handed, I notice that Sam has six neatly arranged fish in his lap, in two rows. I run to the front of the hotel, and then through mud to the street. I can't find Janet, and wonder if I ever will again.

In my analysis of this dream, Janet and I are in an unfamiliar place, similar to a strange city we recently visited together, only now this is psychological territory. We are "ready to come home," to return to the deepest roots of our being with the birth of her child. But there are conflicts to resolve: I must return for my white running suit, which becomes a disguise for "dirty laundry" that Janet apparently does not wish to be made public. What is this dirty laundry? I remember the sexual curiosity I had when I was three years old and my brother was born. In my dream, I think Janet will be angry, just as my mother was when she discovered my intense interest in the origin of the new baby. Will Janet reject me as my mother did?

And Sam and the fish? The fish probably represent sperm, suggesting I knew about conception from my brother's birth.

To look for the package in my dream, and to get to my daughter, I must run through long halls and many rooms, like those I once visited in the monastery of Taormina in Sicily, suggesting I must do penance for my "crimes." But I never find the white suit of my purity. It is gone forever.

❦

April 18

I AM BEGINNING TO REALIZE the origin of my dream fears. I'm afraid I'll "lose" my daughter after the birth of her child, as I "lost" my mother when my brother was born. At that time, too, there was an upheaval in all aspects of my life. Mother, father, sister, grandparents, all neglected me for the new prince. I tried to make sense of my bereavement. I had been a "bad child", I decided, an angry child, a jealous child, a curious child, a sexual child. So I spent my life trying to be "good" to avoid the excruciating feeling of abandonment.

Now I'm terrified of a repeat performance, that I'll lose my place in Janet's family as I did in my own, that I'll lose my wonderful daughter, perhaps my dearest friend. Will she decide I wasn't the mother she thought I was, that she can do it better?

A memory occurs to me. I was singing at a party when I was five years old. "That's enough now," I was told. "Sit down and let your brother sing." Are my singing days with my daughter over, too? Will I lose my importance in her life? Will the interests we share with each other fade into the background?

With my own mother there was room for only one confidant, my sister, and one baby, my brother. Since both positions were filled, there was no place for me to grow into. Is it possible for my daughter and me to find a new relationship to replace the close one we had? Time is short. In my dream, I can have only five minutes (the brief

Dreams and Reality

7

life span left to me), according to the cabby, who looks like my dead husband, Rudy.

I am late returning to the scene, representing my feeling that I am old to be a first-time grandmother. That I can't find Janet and wonder how I'll ever locate her in a strange city suggests I'm afraid I won't recognize this new young mother who is my daughter. Our relationship will certainly change. And if my past experiences are any indication, the change will not be for the better.

But becoming a grandmother, you say, surely that is a spot to fill that didn't exist before. Still, there is the child's other set of grandparents to consider. Will I have to compete with them for my grandchild's affections? Generous, kind, and loving, also rich, they will be some competition. I retain the feelings of the middle child I was. It's hard to believe I won't be crowded out again.

And how about my other children and their spouses? Will they be jealous of the new parents? The new child? Will I have to go through their sibling rivalry all over again? The rivalry that never really stopped? I had to laugh to myself tonight when I noticed my coffee table, on which three photograph albums of the weddings of my children are stacked. I never reshuffle the albums, not caring who's on top. Nevertheless, after each visit of one of my children I always find his or her album is the highest one.

And what about Sam? So far, I've felt lucky to have him in the family, to the point of feeling sometimes that he is another one of my children. As a couple, he and Janet have brought joy into my life. But given his large ego, will I be dissatisfied with the way he parents my grandchild?

On Becoming a Grandparent

Probably. I hope we don't become disillusioned with each other. And what about our visits, our holidays together, our long phone conversations?

Yes, my relationship with Janet and Sam will have to change, as the balance of affections shifts to make room for the new arrival. But wait. I'm very comfortable with my life now. I've reached a hard-won equilibrium and contentment that has taken almost 50 years to achieve. I have wonderful work, enough money, loving children and friends. Do I want or need to be realigned at this late date?

♣

May 1

THE DAM HAS CRACKED. Finally I'm crying, feeling. Remembering my long-gone mother and my father who was once the most important person in my life. I'm mourning for my husband, who died too soon to share this experience with me, who will never see his grandchild. I'm crying as I remember my own babies and my mistakes. But as I think of Janet, happily pregnant, I can wipe away my tears. I must always keep in mind that a new bloom is emerging from the sere leaves of autumn, and life is beginning again.

CHAPTER

II

Changing Patterns

TODAY MY WORLD got a rocket launch. The fetus has become a baby. Janet sent me a sonogram inscribed, "Your grandchild's first pictures."

It's fascinating how modern medicine has penetrated the womb, helping us to one-up nature. The technological tour de force is filled with lines, waves, and shadows. I peer with dispassionate interest, scientifically noting an arc here, a space there. Out of the whirling murk, the head of a three-and-a-half-month-old fetus forms, shaped remarkably like Janet's when she was a newborn. "Baby" is not just an abstract idea now; this is the real thing.

My father had promised me a baby brother for Christmas when I was three years old. Christmas came and went, and there by my bed sat only a doll on a rocking chair. My father, whom I loved more than anyone, had betrayed me. I knew I would never trust anyone again. Then unexpectedly, two weeks later, a baby's cries pierced the darkness. Suddenly the room was full of light. "Daddy, Daddy," I joyfully exclaimed, "It's a real one! It's a real one!" Father could be believed in after all. And Janet has been equally generous. Another "real one" is on the way.

♣

May 12

TECHNOLOGY CHANGES PSYCHOLOGY. When I was pregnant, my babies weren't human to me until I held them in my arms. Now parents can see images of their unborn. Surely that will change their relationship with the child, make the bonding primordial in ways we cannot imagine. And I have viewed a grandchild who has been in my daughter's womb for only three and a half months. I brood about it, daydream about our future relationship, and look forward to greeting this newly implanted being.

I am a doctor of philosophy. My degree is in research, which I come to naturally. Whenever I'm off on a new venture, my custom is to begin reading about the topic. The new knowledge reassures me about the terrors of the unknown, even as I am learning. For example, I spent my first pregnancy reading about the exigencies of childbirth, which scares so many young mothers. Now that my daughter is pregnant, I take to the books once more, to keep up with the growth of the embryo.

I find that the baby is now approximately six inches long. How he or she has grown! Kick and float and feel the swell in your muscles, wriggle and stretch and bask in the glorious sensate peace, that profound shortlived quiescence where freedom is all and no demands are made. Enjoy the first stirrings of the miracle of consciousness. After all, you can cry, frown, squint, and grimace; you can move quickly if your scalp is tickled, react violently to cold water, and double your rate of swallowing if saccharine is injected into the amniotic fluid. That you prefer certain sounds, sights, smells, and tastes and avoid others would seem to be a confirmation of your consciousness. Rejoice, relish, luxuriate in the wonder of it. Wallow in your mother's house. For the rest of your life, you'll long to go back home.

♣

May 13

MUCH AS I LOVE research, psychology was not my first choice of profession. When I was a teenager, I wanted desperately to be an actress. I thought I had to understand people to be able to act them. So I became a psychology major at Temple University in Philadelphia, and I graduated with distinction. But the need to be an actress still drove me, so I put psychology aside and went to New York to study acting at the American Theatre Wing.

By coincidence, Rudy Bond, whom I had known through the Neighborhood Players in Philadelphia, had also enrolled in the American Theatre Wing. He had been the leading man of the Players, when I was an usher at the age of fifteen.

An "older man" of twenty-five, he was direct, honest, vigorous, and the most masculine man I had ever dated. Only one word did him justice, and that word was *sexy.* And he clearly was a man who could deliver what he promised.

We met again outside the Theatre Wing on our first day in New York, and I never again dated another man. We became engaged that week. It was 1947, and I was 24 years old.

My career as an actress was not very successful, especially in comparison with Rudy's. I was a little ingenue who looked like all the others. Strong and rugged, Rudy looked like no one but himself. Soon he was accepted as the first member of the Actors' Studio, and cast in the part of Marlon Brando's friend in the original production of *A Streetcar Named Desire*. I, on the other hand, managed to get three walk-on parts, all wheedled for me by Rudy.

The night *Streetcar* opened, Irene Selznick, the producer, gave a party for Tennessee Williams and the cast at Lindy's. When she introduced me to Elia Kazan as "Rudy's pretty little wifey" I knew I could not go through life as anyone's little wife. My talented husband, whom I loved, was in a Broadway play, and I was getting nowhere. The situation made me ill.

I stayed home for more than a year and read analytic books in the attempt to cure myself. One of the books was Karen Horney's *Self Analysis*. Someone once said that book brought more people into analysis than any other in history. Add me to the list.

Self analysis didn't help me, but the year of reading rekindled my interest in psychology. I enrolled in a psychology program at New York University, and I received a master's degree 15 months later.

At that time, no nonmedical students were accepted as candidates for degrees in psychoanalysis. Then one day

I received a fateful phone call from a friend, who casually said that the National Psychological Association for Psychoanalysis had just opened and was accepting nonmedical applicants for training. I went to the school the next day and enrolled that semester.

I was 27 years old when I first went to an analyst. By then I had been plagued with painful thoughts for fully two years. I had never told anyone, even my husband, about my suffering. Looking back, I can see that it was especially my husband I needed to conceal it from. After all, his talent was the trigger that had set off my distress. (I know now my illness was worse than I'd thought. In one of the first dreams I recorded, a crazy woman was about to attack me with a knife. I didn't realize it at the time, but now I know that the "crazy woman" was me.) One day I had to admit I couldn't heal myself without help. I made an appointment with Dr. B, a motherly, charismatic, Viennese refugee recommended by the school. The fee was ten dollars an hour. I thought it was exorbitant.

I lay shivering on the couch the entire first session, as I told her the story of my life. I cried as I related that I had been married for two years and had given up my profession. To make matters worse, I told Dr. B, my husband was a successful actor cast in the greatest hit of the era. To my surprise, I felt better immediately, and my symptoms disappeared within a matter of weeks.

I learned that the situation in my marriage was reminiscent of the one I had experienced growing up. I had been raised with a favored brother who got everything I wanted. Or at least it felt that way to me. He died of cerebral meningitis when I was 21. Rudy's success aroused my jealousy much as my brother had when I was a child. I was terrified of the power of my wishful thinking (all unconscious, of course) and feared that somehow the killer inside me would murder my husband, too.

My analysis ended successfully five years later. I was then a happily married mother of three, studying for my doctorate at Columbia University, securely and successfully ensconced in the practice of psychoanalysis.

❦

May 25

ACCORDING TO MY READING, it will be at twelve to thirteen weeks that we can first hear the fetal heartbeat with the Doppler ultrasound instrument. Big as a grasshopper, Janet's baby's heart already is beating 120 to 160 times per minute. My heart is beating in time, with pleasure at the thought.

I have also discovered that Janet's fetus is very busy practicing its newfound skills. Now it floats peacefully; now it kicks vigorously; it turns somersaults, hiccups, sighs, urinates, swallows, and "breathes" amniotic fluid; it sucks its thumb, fingers, and toes, grabs its umbilicus, gets excited at sudden noises, calms down when the mother talks quietly, and gets rocked back to sleep as she walks about.

The fetus is already beginning to resemble a complete human being. Its head is now about one-third of its body length. Ribs are clearly visible. Although the baby's eyelids are grown together, not to open until the seventh month, the black pigment of the retina shimmers through the delicate skin. With its large, rounded forehead, lilliputian nose, and well-defined chin, the tiny face has already assumed a human profile. Miniature ears are beginning to form. Nailbeds are firmly embedded in little fingers, and muscles are flexing energetically beneath the skin. Its lips open and close, its forehead wrinkles, its brows rise, and its head turns. And with all this, the new-formed being weighs but three-quarters of an ounce, the weight of an ordinary letter!

At the same time, development is taking place inside the fetus's mouth. Ten tooth buds already are beginning to form in its jaws. Although they won't break through the gums until the baby is five months old, they are lying there waiting for feasts to come. Taste buds are probably already at work, according to a study that involved microscopic examinations of 70 fetal tongues. Since swallowing begins at about 12 weeks, our baby in all likelihood is tasting glucose, fructose, citric acid, and a dozen other substances that have been identified in amniotic fluid. He or she is probably enjoying the sensations, as it has been observed that the fetus has a much larger and wider distribution of taste buds than either the child or the adult. In our family of passionate eaters, this baby's taste buds should have a long and glorious career.

The sense of smell also is beginning to develop, according to another study that found fetuses to exhibit unmistakable facial reactions to various odors. I think it is amusing that newborn infants, with no previous experience with odors, already show preferences. They particularly like the smell of bananas, strawberries, and vanilla, and reject the odor of fish and rotten eggs. Sounds just like my likes and dislikes. Will this child be born with the taste buds of its grandmother? I always thought my father and I had the same food preferences.

The cartilage that make up the fetus's larynx, or voice box, is now forming at the upper end of the windpipe. The vocal cords will not be evident until later. In fact, they will not look completely finished until the infant is six months old.

How will you use them, baby? Will you like to talk when you are little? How about when you grow up? Will you be like one of us? Your Uncle Zane never stopped talking when he was a baby, but he isn't so verbose now. He spends more of his time thinking than talking, and this complements his wife's quiet demeanor. Zane is becoming more and more like his father. For an actor, Rudy was a quiet person, although he had no trouble talking to me. As a matter of fact, we're not a family of great talkers. Janet and Jonathan are often silent, too. I personally do not like chitchat and find cocktail parties a nightmare, although I can talk indefinitely with intimate friends. I am more of a listener, which is compatible with my profession.

In fact, I have experienced close to 35 years of almost nonstop listening. Is it surprising that now I want to speak? Child, will you, like your grandmother, need to develop the "voice" of the writer so you can be heard?

Although there is nothing for the fetus to digest until after birth, the stomach and liver cells that produce digestive juices already are in the process of formation. In digestive systems, too, our extensive family has done well. Except for intestinal cancer late in the life of my Uncle

Emil, and some anal retentiveness in Grandpa Rudy, this portion of the anatomy has functioned beautifully down through our generations. I hope this little one follows suit. For those who might posit that this is a most unaesthetic wish for a grandchild, I'd like to state most emphatically that life can be ruined by a poor digestive tract.

❧

May 26

MY MIND WANDERS from fetal development to sex. Ah, sex! It's hard to believe this little minnow someday will be a sexual person. What would I want sexually for this unborn child? Most of all, I would like to see a lack of precocious sexuality, a slow development at the proper time, with no premature awakenings, seductions, or sexual trauma to keep the child either stuck in primitive forms of gratification or forever immune to the joys of sexuality.

I don't like the permissiveness of the present day. Many of my women patients have told me the same story: embarrassed at being virgins, they "decided" in college it was time to have a sexual experience. So they hopped into bed with the first available date. As a result they experienced no pleasure at all.

I like what happened to me better. First of all, my parents told me very little about sex and left me pretty much to discover it on my own. In contrast to the advice given by most professionals, I have always been grateful that my parents didn't interfere. We know that eating and toilet training proceed better when the child is permitted to behave in accordance with his or her inner needs. Otherwise these functions, in an emotional sense, will seem to "belong" to the parents, and can cause neuroses later on. When parents are too intrusive in the sex lives of their children, a similar takeover can occur. (In keeping with my laid-back philosophy, I tried to keep a respectful distance from the sex lives of my own children. If they wanted to talk about sex, fine. Otherwise I remained silent. Now, in the day of AIDS, this would no longer be as sound. But it worked very well for me then, and I haven't received any complaints.)

In my adolescence, we played kissing games at parties. It wasn't very passionate. In fact, I don't remember any pleasure at all. My friend Bob once told me that most of the fun in kissing games came in the aftermath, when the boys would rejoin the party swooning, buckling at the knees, or gasping in mock excitement. Then everyone would clap or laugh depending on the intensity of the boy's reaction.

It was with Bob, an "older man" of 20, that I experienced my first real kiss. I was 16. Bob was in love with me. He had just taken me for my first sailboat ride, in the days when men paid their date's way. We were sitting on a bench on the boardwalk at the Inlet in Atlantic City. I remember the hardness of the bench, the feel of the gentle spray of the ocean, the smell of the salt-laden night. He kissed me all over my face, and each kiss sent a ripple of electricity through my body. I hadn't known such pleasure existed. There was a whole new color added to the world's spectrum.

Bob and I were together for four years, and step by

step he led me deeper into the realms of sensuality. Each move forward was an exciting battle in which I resisted, fought to hold my ground, and gave way. Perhaps it was because he loved me, or because of our lingering exploration of each other, or perhaps it was his gifts as a lover. But the pleasurable, leisurely tempo kept me from being overwhelmed. If I had been a child of the sixties, I am sure I would have had problems. As it is, sex has always been one of the exquisite joys of my life. Baby, that's the way I'd like it to be for you.

Bob was my intellectual as well as sensual mentor. He was the first person I knew who told me I was intelligent. He taught me about music, art, and science, and brought me books such as *Zuleika Dobson* and *The Ordeal of Richard Feverel*. I don't think I would have had the courage to go to college if it hadn't been for Bob's support. He probably had the greatest influence on my thinking of anyone in my life, next to Freud. I hope what I learned from Bob will help to shape the intellectual environment of my grandchild.

♣

May 27

THIS MAKES ME WONDER what kind of profession the baby will follow. Love and work are all that matter, Freud said. If you are capable of the two, you will be emotionally healthy. As a child I dreamed of both. When I was 11 years old I wrote a poem in which I dreamed of what I would be when I grew up. It was childish and badly rhymed, but my ambition, even then, was manifest. The first lines read:

On Becoming a Grandparent

When all the world is sleeping sound
My pencil is writing and my head's going round.
I rack my brains for things to come
And if I'm lucky there are sure to be some.

I didn't do badly with my ambitions. I was an actress for a while, and I even acquired a piece or two of glamorous jewelry. I never became president, but I have circled the earth a number of times. I have a reputable profession and have even managed to become a writer. And now my grandchild's mind is beginning to develop. Who knows what potential is slumbering in that smidgen of protoplasm?

Janet has always been less ambitious than I. Already she's decided to put her child first. Unlike me, she does not want to have a full-time practice, but says she will be satisfied to work part-time. When she was a little girl, I asked her if she would like to be a genius. "I don't want to *be* a genius," she answered. "I'd like to *marry* a genius." I was the other way around, an anomaly in my time. I came from a background in which ambition leads to success. Children of immigrants are always ambitious. For our children, safe and secure financially, it is not so important. Probably Janet's baby will feel the same way.

But still . . . What wondrous possibilities are in store for this little grasshopper! Perhaps he or she will be a professor of literature or even a Nobel Prize winner. How about a doctor who discovers the cure for cancer? Or a Supreme Court justice? A violinist or pianist also would do nicely.

I know it isn't very likely he or she will be a genius. Genetics are important, and most members of our family are pretty ordinary, although I've occasionally heard the word applied to Rudy and Jonny, and even, if I may brag a bit, to myself, namely when my ninth-grade English teacher said a composition I wrote showed "a touch of genius," and when a friend commented, "Alma has a genius for living." But we don't hold a candle to the family of Virginia Woolf, for example, in which geniuses appeared regularly in generation after generation, and in which the constant presence of greatness nurtured the developing artists.

Experience has taught me that health is far more important than accomplishment. (After all, Virginia Woolf, for all her genius, committed suicide.) And if the baby turns out to be an ordinary mortal like the rest of us, I'll love him or her just as much. But I can dream, can't I? I'll settle for living long enough to encourage the spark.

♣

May 28

APPARENTLY I'M NOT THE ONLY DREAMER HERE. Research suggests that the baby already may be dreaming at this early stage of its life. Scientists believe that dream activity originates in the pons varolii, a band of nerve fibers in the brain that connects the lobes of the midbrain, medulla oblongata, and cerebrum. Thus there is no physical reason why dreams cannot occur early in gestation and include material from the fetus's previous experience. Of course it makes one wonder what there possibly could be for the baby to dream about. If all dreams contain a wish, and if returning to the womb is seen in the unconscious as the essence of paradise, what would the fetus dream of? A return to nonexistence, perhaps? A total nothingness? Perhaps, if one agrees with Freud's concept of the death instinct, in which the basic wish of all human beings is to return to the inanimate state.

Here's a new thought. Dr. Thomas Verny believes that the fetus may even be able to tune into the dreams of the mother, so that her dreams become the baby's dreams. I don't know if I'd like that. It would be like having your mental telephone tapped.

☙

June 19

"MOMMY," JANET SAYS ON THE PHONE, "I'm worried."

"What's the matter?"

"Shouldn't I feel life already? I'm 19 weeks pregnant."

My heart sinks. "Well," I reassure her, "You saw the baby moving in the sonogram."

"Yes," she answers, "but that was weeks ago."

"Maybe it's a gentle baby," I say, "A nice quiet girl like you were."

"Well, I do have the funniest feeling inside, though," she continues.

"Like what?" I ask eagerly.

"Like, well, oh, I can't explain. Like something is twitching around inside me, but I can't be sure!"

A surge of pure joy. "That's it! That's it! I remember, I remember! That's the way it was with me! I had this funny little feeling, gentle as could be, maybe like gas, but

Changing Patterns

23

I couldn't be sure. It got stronger and stronger. And then it turned into a baby. Don't be surprised if you get poked in the stomach some time real soon." I laugh with relief.

♣

July 1

I HAD ANOTHER DREAM last night. I'm living in a new house. It is white, with columns in the front; the kind of house I had fantasies of living in when I was a child. I have just moved in; the plaster on the walls is not yet dry. Without my permission, a motion picture company has taken it over to make a film. They are moving around the furniture, beds, pictures, and other household paraphernalia. I feel bewildered and unable to stop them. A young and handsome man is in charge. He looks like my son Jonathan but is grumpy like Humphry, the most talented character in *The Common Pursuit,* a play by Simon Gray I saw several years ago. Someone says the man is older than the others, but he looks very young to me.

In the dream, I am having a terrible time getting dressed. I put on one thing and another, and either the skirt is too tight or I cannot find the right blouse because it is in another room, where a group of women psychoanalysts are having a meeting. I am supposed to see a patient for analysis in an early session, but am unable to get there.

After much struggle I finally manage to arrive at my office. Unlike my real one, the office door in my dream is on the side of the house. The patient is waiting. She is wearing a black and white outfit.

The fact that in the dream I moved into a splendid new house reminds me that Janet and Sam don't like the four-room apartment in Manhattan where I've been living since Rudy died. They want me to move to more elegant quarters and say they will even come to New York to find a better apartment and move me into it. But I'm very comfortable here and in my office on the ground floor. Both places are simple to take care of and I like going to work on the elevator, instead of using subways or taxis. I enjoy having Central Park on one side and Madison Avenue on the other, so I can run in one and shop on the other.

As you enter my living room, you pass through a small foyer in which there are huge blown-up snapshots of my family from 20 years ago, including our dog, Ginger. Over the pictures hangs an acrylic shelf on which there are 14 clay figures molded by me 10 or 12 years ago. The living room walls are paneled in walnut, as are the ubiquitous book shelves filled with psychoanalytic books, so that it resembles a library more than a living room.

Sheltered by the bookshelves is a mahogany rolltop desk that is full of all kinds of little nooks and crannies. Rudy and I bought it at the Salvation Army for 35 dollars when we were first married.

Scattered around the room are colorful rugs I brought back from India and China. A carved wooden and glass curio cabinet contains little treasures given me by my children and friends, as well as those collected in a lifetime of traveling. The entire end of the room fronting the street is filled with plants.

I love this room. It is a perfect reflection of me and all my selves: wife, mother, friend, psychoanalyst, writer, sculptor, and traveler; vain, pretentious, yearning, nostalgic, sentimental, comfort-seeking, extravagant and penny-pinching, perfectionist and careless. Or at least I thought it was perfect until I had this dream of moving into a mansion like Tara!

My dream also contained direct memories of my own pregnancy. A pregnant patient of mine once said, "I am somebody's house!" During pregnancy, that "house" is occupied and taken over by another. Once the "tenant" moves in, life goes on inside the dwelling without the permission of the "landlady."

The dream probably was triggered by Janet's call the other night. She feels different physically these days, as if she's living in someone else's body. "It took so many years to get acquainted with what makes me comfortable," she said. "Like what I need to eat. Now I have totally different tastes in food. I've always loved chocolate. Now I don't like it at all. I love vegetables, but can't stand the thought of eating them. The other day I felt guilty about not consuming any, so I decided to make myself eat carrots. Would you believe that ten minutes later I threw up? I get all these weird yeast infections I've never had before. And I have a black line, from my belly button all the way down, that I don't care for! And hairy! And I get jealous of all these cute figures wearing jeans. I feel like I'll be pregnant forever!"

I remember having similar feelings during my pregnancies. Every aspect of me changed. My body, of course, remodeled itself. Clothes fit badly, if at all. My face changed too. It became softer, more tranquil friends said. Movement slowed down. I had to learn to navigate myself differently, judging space as if I were driving a new car. Unlike most pregnant women, I ate less than usual, and after delivery I was 10 or 15 pounds lighter than before conception. (When I gained weight a few years later, a friend quipped, "It's time to have another baby.") Sleep became heavy, as if in a fever or a heavily drugged state. Revolutionized bathroom habits made me a permanent tenant. Unknown liquids oozed from my orifices. My own smells became unfamiliar. Usually volatile and active, I became a placid armchair dreamer. Even the omnipresent book fell unread into my lap.

To my surprise, my new passivity made me a better analyst. I became a better listener. But personal moods altered. I frequently broke into tears with family and friends. I was living in a "new house," which was wonderful and terrible at the same time.

Cigarettes tasted and smelled like garbage, so I stopped smoking, in the days when everyone smoked. Since then, scientific evidence has indicated that a mother's cigarette smoking is disastrous for the fetus, who grows agitated whenever the mother even thinks of having a cigarette. It is strange that the fetus reacts as forcefully to the mother's thoughts of smoking as it does to the actual deed, but apparently it has access to her thinking. The agitation is caused by a drop in its oxygen supply, as smoking lowers the oxygen content of the maternal blood passing through the placenta.

My dream shouts of internal uproar. I'm going through a brand-new move (the plaster on the walls is not yet dry); in fact, a double pregnancy, with Janet's baby and this diary. I'm worried about the public exposure of my

Changing Patterns

27

most private feelings. Speaking of exposure, I remember being embarrassed at being pregnant. It was as if I were making a public statement to the world, "Look what I've been doing!"

I have decided I don't like being thought of primarily as a grandmother. Last night at the Institute for Psychoanalytic Training and Research meeting it was announced that my daughter is going to give birth in November and that therefore we had to change the date of a workshop scheduled to be given at that time. It was flattering to have everyone so interested, but I don't know if I'm ready yet for that kind of attention. I feel too young. At various times of my life, I've thought of myself as daughter, sister, student, friend, lover, wife, mother, psychoanalyst, writer. That's who I've been up till now. Yet here I am keeping a diary to establish myself in yet another identity. The idea is so overwhelming I can't get it all together (the clothes are scattered in my dream.) I will have to rework every important aspect of my present life as well as the past (pregnancies, early history, relationships, deaths and losses), to become whole again on this new level.

In analyzing my dream, I believe I had trouble reaching my patient because neither she nor I can "get it all together." She is a new mother whose father is dying. She wears white and black, the colors of innocence and mourning. We were both "Daddy's girls." The dream suggests that both of us must work through further grief for our fathers to successfully navigate these difficult new waters. Perhaps I haven't done well enough at this for either one of us yet. The office door has been moved to the side of the house, which graphically indicates that psycho-analysis no longer is central in my life, at least for the time being.

In my dream, a man like Jonathan is in charge. Of my three children, Jonny is the most like me in appearance and temperament. One of my favorite jokes (or is it a wish?) is that if I were a 29-year-old man, I would look just like him. I think in the dream Jonny stands for the masculine side of me that is causing all the commotion. The aspect of me that Jonny represents doesn't want children; his priority in life is getting on with his career. He is grumpy, as I have been lately, without really know-ing why. He is my virtuoso self, who will help me "get it together", as "he" always has before. For just as Humphry is the most talented and efficient character in *The Com-mon Pursuit,* my professional self is the most gifted aspect of me. And I'm resisting the change.

But in the dream I've succeeded in moving to a new house, the kind in which "I've always wanted to live." It is a white house, free of impurities. (It seems I have worked through the "dirty linen" of the April seventeenth dream.) This move has cost a great deal. I have toiled long and hard both inside and out of my office to get where I am. But the work is not finished. There is always an upheaval after a move to a new home. It is understandable that chaos would follow a psychological move as well. I must sort through the chaos and see who I am now, and who I am becoming. But I am fighting the "remodeling." I say to myself, why the resistance? Why not enjoy the process?

♣

I VISITED JANET AND SAM this Fourth of July weekend. He is very interested in my diary project and says he is going to write down all *his* dreams. He has already had a dream in which the baby is a boy, nine months old and already talking to him. Sam says he is a little intimidated by the idea of caring for a newborn infant and would feel more secure with a somewhat older baby. I suspect, too, that he is jealous that the baby can communicate with Janet, through its movement in her body, but not with him. If the child of the dream is nine months old, then he can "talk" to Sam too.

♣

July 10

SAM IS GETTING OVER HIS FEAR of the newborn. His latest dream concerns Janet breastfeeding the new baby. (Of course, his various dreams could be a kind of therapy for him. This is something I didn't anticipate.)

At any rate, Sam says that in his dream Janet is having trouble feeding the infant. "She is restless and isn't feeding it right," he says. "I wanted to make sure the baby got fed. I had to move it around from boob to boob. I kept saying 'Let's try the other one.' After three or four moves, it worked. Janet calmed down after the baby got what it needed."

Janet laughed and said, "Isn't that just like Sam? He always has to do everything himself. He's the kind of person who takes the word of no authority. A few months ago his cousin Zack was flying us in his plane to Rum Cay in the Bahamas, and Sam gave Zack directions. Never-mind that he knows nothing about flying a plane and we got lost and landed in Nassau instead of Eleuthera."

We're trying to get Sam's parents to save *their* dreams about the baby, but they're not being very cooperative. A few months ago Sam's father, Harry, told me a dream in which he was moving backward, and asked what I thought about it. Since he asked, I told him I thought he wanted to return to the time when he was a little boy. But apparently he was upset by my comment. He said, "I'm not going to dream anymore, if that's what it means!"

❧

July 12

JANET CALLED TO TELL ME she went to the doctor today. She and the baby are doing well, except that she has put on 13 pounds in five months. The doctor said she must stop gaining, immediately. Sam and I are getting heavier, too. It seems we all are pregnant.

But . . . the baby is a breech. I turn to the latest edition of *The Merck Manual,* which says, "The primary problem with breech presentation is that the soft parts of the lower portion of the body and trunk can mold to fit through the pelvis, but the head has no chance to undergo molding. Thus disproportion is not discovered until the body has been delivered and the head is caught. These infants may die." For the safety of baby, Janet probably will need a Caesarean section. She is cheerful about it. Although she still is preparing for natural childbirth, she says she cares only that the baby is born healthy.

Janet is a lot more sensible than her mother was. My first child, Zane, was also a breech. Natural childbirth was new in those days, and I was very excited about it. I had prepared intensively and had chosen my physician in large measure because he had said he would cooperate. At the beginning of labor, he gently informed me that because of the position of the child, the birth would take longer than most. Innocent that I was 36 years ago, this did not alarm me. My labor continued for 24 hours with me valiantly doing breathing exercises, getting nowhere. The doctor finally retreated. He gave me a spinal block, and delivered my child himself. He said later that he had not wanted to deprive me of the joy of being conscious at the moment of my child's birth. He should have. According to *Merck*, "Brain damage due to anoxia [lack of oxygen] is markedly increased in breech presentation." Zane didn't breathe for a full minute after his birth, with a ring of physicians hovering over him until his belated first cry. There is no doubt that he should have been delivered by cesarean, and he would be if he were delivered today. I feel the long and difficult labor was responsible for the severe reading disability Zane struggled with for much of his life. Although some authorities believe that neurological difficulties contribute to difficulties in learning, a precise understanding of brain-behavior relationships still lies in the future. Nevertheless, although Zane disagrees with me, I have always felt guilty that my insistence on natural childbirth was responsible for a possible minimal brain dysfunction.

I remember my mother's guilt over not having prevented my brother's death, even though neither doctors nor penicillin could save him. There are some things for which we always blame ourselves, whether we are technically guilty or not.

Still, Zane is luckier than my Aunt Helen's child of 66 years ago. That child was a breech, too. It had to be removed piece by piece from Helen's womb, in order to save her life.

♣

July 14

JANET IS REMAINING CALM, but the pregnancy seems to have made her nostalgic for her childhood. For example, we were talking about a story I had written for her and her brother as children, "The Tree That Could Fly." As I recalled the first line, "Once upon a time there was a fairy called Bluey, because her wings were blue as the sky," Janet's eyes filled with tears. Now she wants me to look up the story and get it ready as a gift for my grandchild.

♣

July 15

SPEAKING OF CRYING, research tells us that babies also cry in the womb, a condition known as vagitus uterinus. It has been said that if the uterus were filled with air instead of amniotic fluid, one could hear the fetus crying much of the time. Are you crying now, baby? I'm sorry. It must be very lonely with no one to console you. I never liked to hear my babies cry. My husband always said I awoke just *before* my babies cried. I wish I could pick you up and comfort you, as I did them.

Changing Patterns

By this time, the auditory apparatus of the unborn baby is as developed as that of a grown-up. With the aid of acoustic spectrograms that yield "cryprints" as unique as fingerprints, scientists have discovered that fetuses are receiving and storing characteristics of their mothers' speech, as well as her heartbeat and the "rhythmical whooshing sound of the mother's bloodflow punctuated by the tummy rumbles of air passing through his mother's stomach and the noise and rhythm of her breathing." Further studies seem to indicate that the fetus moves in rhythm with the mother's speech. Babies of mute mothers were found to cry strangely or not at all, as if they'd missed their lessons in the womb. Janet's baby already knows and recognizes her voice! S/he likes music, too. Janet says the baby is quiet when she talks or when Vivaldi or Mozart is playing on the stereo. According to other prenatal research, the fetuses studied liked the music of those composers, as indicated by their steady heartbeats and absence of movement. But they kicked violently when Brahms, Beethoven, and all forms of rock were played.

So here we have a miniature person with a beating heart, who floats, dives, kicks, and flexes, sees, hears, tastes, smells, cries, has distinctive fingerprints, exhibits facial expressions, urinates, can get excited and be reassured, has rudimentary teeth and larynx, stomach and liver cells that produce digestive juices, functioning kidneys, and, if the child is a boy, a developed penis. This baby may even dream. A complete human being lies waiting in my daughter's womb. Dear little unknown one, we are waiting, too.

On Becoming a Grandparent

Matinee and Evening Performance

July 19

MY DAUGHTER-IN-LAW Wendy is pregnant, too! Wendy and Jonny came for an overnight visit on her return from a business trip to Florence. When I mentioned Janet's pregnancy Wendy reponded, "You're going to have two grandchildren."

"What?" I stammered, displaying a lack of cool as well as originality. "You mean you're going to have a baby, too?" Gush of joy and excitement. Hugs. Kisses.

"I'm six weeks pregnant now."

"And you thought you'd have trouble conceiving."

"No, it was easy."

Jonny is beaming, proud of his achievement. He is my baby, five minutes younger than Janet.

Wendy is glowing; she has a luminescent look. When she first came in, I said, "You look wonderful. Your buying trip must have agreed with you." She gave me her Mona Lisa smile. I should have realized the truth then. "You'll have more to write about now," she said with a grin.

Before Wendy and Jonny went off to sleep, I said, "Don't forget to remember any dreams about having a baby."

The next morning Wendy said, "I dreamed I had a dream about having a baby, and then I dreamed I forgot it."

I think it is safe to say she has mixed feelings about being a subject for this diary.

♣

July 20

I'M IMPROVING. I must be getting used to the idea of being a grandmother. All the guilt, fear, and memories I've begun to work out about Janet and Sam's baby will probably make it easier to accept the existence of this new one without so much emotional tumult.

Right now, in contrast to my initial "freeze" at Janet's phone announcement, I feel many emotions all at once. I experience a strange pulling in my head, as if it were too full to absorb all my sensations. I'm trying to "pull down" some of them, so I can deal with what is left. I'm unsuccessful. I sleep very badly at night.

While tossing around in bed, I realize that part of the problem is this diary. I've pretty much had it mapped out in my head to follow the intrauterine development of one baby and the psychological changes it causes in everyone concerned. But two babies? How can I work in this new development? In this case, 1 and 1 seems to make 22.

What if Jonny and Wendy produce twins? I did, and I know it's economical emotionally as well as financially. Giving birth to my two infants at one time seemed a bonus. As my husband said at their birth, "We sure hit the jackpot!" The "jackpot" has expanded as these two babies have grown to adulthood.

To be honest, though, raising twins is not an unmitigated blessing. From birth on, difficulties don't simply add up with two babies; they multiply. One child rarely let me complete an action fully before the other asked for attention. Feeding two infants at a time is hardly twice the pleasure of feeding one, but it is more than double the trouble. Which baby do you hold when no one else is around? And how do you enjoy one baby's bath while the other is screaming to be held? Taking a walk with them through city streets often was a matter of life and death. I remember being at the corner of 99th Street and West End Avenue, where we lived when they were toddlers. One baby ran into 99th Street and the other into West End Avenue, at the very same moment!

Worst of all was the rivalry. When the children were two years old, they literally tried to kill each other. Janet stomped on Jonny's head until his eye swelled up like a balloon. Jonny threw a can at Janet's head, which required a seam of stitches to put together again. When I asked my analyst what to do about it, she said, "Don't leave them alone together."

Matinee and Evening Performance

A little later I asked Janet, "Why do you fight so much?" She replied, "When we fight, we're not twins."

The children must have felt the tension in other ways, too. When they were about four, Janet asked, "If you, Jonny, and I were all in a boat together and the boat sank, which one of us would you save?" Before I could answer, she added, "Oh, I know what you'd do. You'd save one of us and get Dad to save the other!" That's what I did with them many times. When both children were hungry, I "got Dad" to feed one; when sleepy, I summoned Dad to tuck one in. With all its disadvantages, I was lucky to be married to an actor who was home at more unconventional times than the usual husband.

Rudy and I had a bedroom with a bathroom on each side. One evening when the twins were a bit older, each was taking a bath in one of the bathrooms. I was lying in bed reading a book. Suddenly both twins began to shout. When I ran to see what the trouble was, each complained I had been in the bathroom with the other too long.

And yet today, all of my three children feel they are my favorite child, secure that they are lovable people. Although it may sound that way, I don't believe there is any self-deception involved. I have the knack of throwing myself into the moment, of returning to the symbiotic union that exists between mother and infant, in which only the "nursing couple" exists. I try to teach both my children and my patients that they, too, can learn to go in and out of this state without getting stuck in it. Otherwise, people are terrified of losing their identity, and are afraid to commit themselves to a deep relationship. When I am with someone I care about, the rest of the world is blocked out. I take them back to the time when they *should have been* the only one in the world for mother, but weren't, and give them a new experience. I think this ability, as much as anything else, helps my patients get well. In this sense, my children are right; at different moments of our lives, we are all a favorite child.

⚜

July 21

AS A CHILD, I wished I had been a twin. A lonely youngster, I never felt accepted by my family. I longed for a person just like me to understand me completely, so I'd never be alone again. Anna Freud said the fantasy of being a twin is nothing at all like the real experience. She was right.

From childhood on, I read everything I could find about twins, starting with the Bobbsey Twins books. One of the reasons I did undergraduate work in psychology at Temple University was to study about twins. Rudy said I wanted them so badly, I finally managed to produce them. I wonder if that's as far-fetched as it sounds. If one can develop an illness like cancer for psychosomatic reasons, who is to say the body can't produce a healthy phenomenon in the same way?

I suspected I was having twins when I was three months pregnant, because I felt two kicks at the same time that were fully 12 inches apart. When I told the doctor about it he said "No, you're not having twins. You simply feel reflected motion."

I got no support for the idea from my analytic

supervisor, either. She said "Oh, no, Alma. You're not having twins. It is just a fantasy." Much later, when the babies were keeping us up night after night, I got my revenge. I wrote her a letter saying, "At three o'clock in the morning when both babies are crying, I say, 'Oh, don't get up, Alma, it's only a fantasy!'"

Only Rudy believed me. He thought it would be terrific to get two babies for the price of one. He was proud of his virility, and believed the accomplishment was all his. In his opinion, the father of twins must be a mighty man. Rudy was a great actor, but a scientist he wasn't. Nevertheless, he was warm and accepting about the idea of having two babies at once. I'll always be grateful for it.

Finally, in my eighth month, an X ray was taken. Sure enough, there were two babies, one nestled behind the other, which was why two heartbeats had not been picked up before. My first reaction was to kiss the doctor. Then I ran to my analyst with great excitement to tell her the wonderful news. Her response was quite sobering. She felt sorry for me. "Twins are terribly difficult to raise," she said. "Usually, at least one of them turns out to be neurotic." Undaunted, I thought, "What's a little neurosis compared with the wonder of two new lives!" I've never really changed my mind about that, despite difficulties and frustrations along the way.

I loved the birth announcements we sent out when the twins were born. The inside of the card said the usual about proudly announcing the arrival of Jonathan and Janet, etc. But the part I really cherished was the front of the card. Conceived by Rudy the actor, it read:

On Becoming a Grandparent

MATINEE

and

EVENING PERFORMANCE

Twenty-nine years later, it seems we are going to have at least two babies at the same time again, another matinee and evening performance. I wish Rudy could be around to see the curtain go up.

♣

July 22

JONNY SURPRISES ME. As a boy, he was puny as well as short, with a high-pitched voice that annoyed everyone. Zane used to call Jonny "the Screecher." But even though he was two feet shorter than his cohorts on the basketball court, his high school coach wrote in his yearbook, "Inch for inch, pound for pound, he is the best athlete in the school."

To watch Jonny work on one of his advertising campaigns is invigorating. In an instant, he has mapped out a plan which would seem to many to require a month to design. Once a friend said that he wanted to marry a woman with a child because, at 44, he felt too old to bring up a baby. Jonny immediately came up with an ad for a personals column: it began, "Too old to start from scratch."

His gifts to me are always original. Jonny seems to know what I want before I want it, an example of the "symbiotic gift," when one person understands the other as well as him- or herself. Like the green running suit he bought me 15 years ago that fit so perfectly. It had never occurred to me that I could be a runner. But if I had a running suit I had to run, right? I haven't stopped since. I run around the reservoir practically every day, rain or shine. A few years ago, I ran several ten-kilometer races and actually won a few medals. I don't put too much stock in them, however, especially the last race. The good news was that I had won third prize in my age group. The bad news was that there were only three people entered in the category.

Now that Jonny is to be a father, I'm sure he will apply his empathetic personality to that task, too. He has already said he wants to be the kind of father who will play ball with his son when the child is 30 years old. He is remembering, I suppose, his own childhood with an "old" father, always too tired or preoccupied to play with his children.

And he has grown to be a loving husband, often holding hands with Wendy, stroking her hair or kissing her. This is another surprise, because he was not an affectionate baby. For his first few years, my unspoken fear was that he was mildly autistic. Or just "cold," as my mother's family was said to be. But I went on holding and stroking him and kissing him whenever I could. I treated him the way he treats Wendy now. This implies to me that Jonny is secure in his masculinity, and not afraid to identify with his mother.

♣

July 22 (later)

WENDY CAME IN wearing an enormous white T-shirt with a picture of a giant embryo on the belly. Her brother Eric had given it to her with a note saying: "Dear Wendy:

I saw this T-shirt and couldn't resist. I hope it's big enough. Sorry that poor baby has to stand on its head the whole nine months!"

Wendy told me she had had a dream she wanted to tell. She began, "My doctor told me he had good news and bad news. The good news was that I was going to have twins. The bad news was that since there were going to be two babies there was a greater chance of losing one of them and I had to be very careful. In the dream, I was ambivalent. I was excited about the idea of having twins, but was angry that I had to be so careful. I was worried that I had come so far and still might lose the baby . . . What do you think it means?"

Wendy's question posed a problem for me. Psychoanalysts are not supposed to give "parlor interpretations," better known as "wild analysis." Before responding, I thought over very carefully whether I should answer with the truth as I saw it. I decided anything else would be insulting. So I answered, "I think the dream concerns your mixed feelings about having a baby. First you were ambivalent about having a child at all. Then you worked it out and were very happy about it. But maybe there is still a bit of the old doubt left. If you had two babies and one died, both your wishes would come true, the wish to have a baby and the wish not to.

"Then, too, twins run in both our families, so there is a very real possibility you might have them. Just as you were ambivalent about having one baby, I think that now you are conflicted about the idea of twins. You would like to have two babies at once. Yet, at the very same time, you wouldn't like it at all."

Matinee and Evening Performance

"Yes," she answered solemnly. "And I don't know if I want a boy or a girl. If I had twins I could have both."

She subsequently had two nightmares, which she also recounted, although with some reluctance after I told her about my diary entries.

"This probably is very typical," she started off. Her comment tells me something very important about Wendy. She is correct; the dream *is* very typical. In fact, it expresses a universal fear of pregnant women that their child will be deficient in some way. What is unusual is that Wendy knows her dream is characteristic. People are notorious deniers when it comes to dreams. For example, a patient whose dreams are discussed in detail in a book of mine called *Dream Portrait* preceded the retelling of a beautiful dream that heralded the end of his long and successful analysis with the comment, "This dream is not very important." But Wendy is realistic; what she sees is what there is. Her judgment is excellent. She is a good counterpart to Jonny, who often spins castles in the clouds.

"I dreamed there was something wrong with the baby," she said. "It was a terrible shock. I remember thinking, 'What am I going to do?' I was furious at the doctor for not giving me the proper tests. And then I woke up."

How can I tell Wendy she is terrified she will bear a retarded child? In the dream, she is trying to prepare herself for that possibility, in order to avoid the shock. Wendy is a loyal person, especially to family. On the one hand, she thinks she could not possibly cope with raising a damaged child. I suspect she worries that a child like that would hamper their beautiful, ambitious lives. On the other hand, she has a powerful conscience that would insist she stand by family whatever the emotional cost. Her dilemma: should she keep such a baby or institutionalize it? Wendy has difficulty making decisions of all kinds, serious or trivial. She agonized for more than a year about whether she wanted to live in New York or near her parents in New Jersey and still hasn't made a permanent commitment. But the possibility of being forced to decide between keeping a retarded child at home and placing the child in an institution is so horrifying it wakes her up. The nightmare presents a problem for which there can be no ideal solution.

"I had another nightmare," Wendy confided, "but this one was funny. I dreamed that even though I was pregnant, we had a choice of either Jonny or me having a Caesarean. He decided to have it. There we were in the hospital, and they were preparing him for surgery. They were doing it very slowly. First they prepped him for the operation. Then when they took him into the operating room, he fainted."

I don't think this nightmare is funny at all. It concerns another terror of Wendy's, and the subject scares me, too. Wendy is petite, 4 feet 11 inches tall at most. Although she appears to have a good-size pelvis, the doctor says she is very small internally. Jonny is 5 feet 8, and Wendy's parents and I all hover around the average in height, too. Nevertheless, the doctor says the baby already weighs about eight pounds. The child must take after Rudy and Zane, the tall members of our family, both of whom reached almost 6 feet. As a result of the discrepancy between the baby's size and Wendy's, there is a good possibility the baby will have to be delivered by Caesarean section. In my interpretation of her dream, she spares herself the terrifying ordeal of the Caesarean as well as the indignity of being "prepped" by having Jonny deliver the baby instead. It is a neat solution. And maybe a funny one at that.

But despite the attempt at humor, this dream is no more successful than the first one. According to Freud, dreams are the preservers of sleep. Sleeping through a dream indicates we have been successful in keeping our anxieties at least temporarily at bay. When a dreamer awakens, it means that the dream has failed in its primary function, that of preserving sleep. The disguises haven't worked, and our anxiety has crashed through our defenses. Even though it is now Jonny being operated on instead of Wendy, her terror breaks through. "Jonny" faints and Wendy becomes so upset she wakes up.

This nightmare reminds me of one Wendy had before she was married. In that dream, as she was walking down the aisle at her wedding, she also fainted. At the time, I asked her if she was frightened of marriage, and she admitted she was. We talked about it, and perhaps it helped, because she performed magnificently at the actual ceremony. But apparently she is even more frightened of having a Caesarean than of getting married; at least in the earlier dream, she was able to picture herself walking down the aisle before she fainted. In the present dream, she removes herself bodily from the situation. Jonny "decides" to have the baby, and Jonny is the one who faints.

When Jonny decides to go through surgery instead of Wendy, I see him as the "good mother." This reminds me again that he treats Wendy the way I treated him as a baby. He does all he can for her, even cleaning up after her when she vomits. A *really* good mother would want to protect Wendy and have the operation for her.

I don't blame Wendy for being terrified. The prospect of a Caesarean, of being cut open by the surgeon's knife, is daunting. Thousands of women feel the same way. She is bearing up beautifully, however. But when I told her I thought she was doing well, she denied it, saying, "You should see how bad-tempered I am around the house."

I'm so worried about both my girls that, when Wendy delegates the Caesarean to Jonny in her dream, I feel she's saying it's not fair for women to have the fear and pain of labor and for men to escape it all. She's going on strike, with a picket sign that reads, "Biology is unfair to women!"

A friend asked me if I feel different about Wendy's giving birth than I do about Janet's. Of course I do, but I fudged a bit in answering. But once again, Wendy has proved to be the realist. "You couldn't possibly feel the same about my pregnancy as you do about Janet's," she said last night. "After all, I'm not your daughter."

No, I don't feel the same about her pregnancy as I do about Janet's. Nor do I think any mother possibly could. The love of one's children, at least for me, is passionate and primitive. The love for one's daughter-in-law, if one is lucky, is much more civilized, the affection one feels for a dear, younger friend.

Matinee and Evening Performance

Mothers and Daughters

August 31

JANET AND SAM just left for the airport after a visit. I am surprised that I am in tears. I welcome the blue feeling, though, for it may get me back to writing about "my" babies. I've been in Europe since July 24, and now that I've returned, I have lost the feeling for writing about them. I'm still very interested in "having" the babies; I drool over every infant I see and buy little outfits everywhere, like the tiny Aran sweaters I brought from Ireland. But somehow the inspiration for writing about the babies has fled. What I do all day now is mope around reading junk books, waiting for the moody muse.

It's irritating, because all I wanted to do before I left for Europe was to write about becoming a grandmother. But my traveling plans had long been set, and there was no way to change them. But here I am with a week to devote to writing before I go back to work, and no inspiration at all.

And there is something worse. I've lost the connection with my first grandchild in his or her sixth month of life.

There was a phone call on my answering machine when I got home last night that made all my years of practice feel worthwhile. A woman said in a hesitating voice, "You probably won't remember me, but this is Miriam H———. I was in treatment with you 30 years ago. I just wanted to tell you how much you helped me and that my life has been better all these years because of you. Thank you and God bless you."

Of course I remember her. She was a warm, friendly, very heavy woman, with a tremendous appetite. She came to analysis because she wanted a child, but was afraid to have one because she had a recurrent fantasy that she roasted a baby in the oven and ate it. After a year or so of treatment, she remembered that when she was very little, her father had played a game with her in which he had said, "I'm going to eat you up." He then pretended to devour every part of her. She remembered being frightened that he really was going to do it. As a result of our work, she put her fears to rest and was able to give birth to a daughter. And no, she didn't eat her up! Just thinking about the call makes me feel better about our own fears.

Janet is fine. She is carrying splendidly. She hasn't gained weight anywhere but in her belly, which is hard and pointed. We went swimming while she was here and I looked over at her in the water. I saw this long slender body skimming along the blue of the water, with a snug little cabin hanging below like the one on a dirigible. Remember the old wives' tale that a pregnant woman with a pointed abdomen is carrying a boy, while the woman displaying a rounded one will give birth to a girl? If there is any truth to the tale, Janet will have a son. Come to think of it, I dreamed last night that she had a boy. The dream was characterized by a glorious medley of color, which some analysts (including me) believe is a prediction of things to come. If color in a dream is really a prophecy, that old wives' tale may be correct . . .

It's weird how much Janet's pregnancy is like mine were, particularly my first. I, too, gained very little weight and carried it all up front. The baby seemed to rest on my stomach, and—for a change—I couldn't eat. People told me the French say a woman really doesn't have a good figure until after she gives birth. That seemed to be true for me. My figure never was better than right after I had a child.

I experienced an uncanny feeling while Janet and I were at the pool. Two women wearing similar caps and one-piece bathing suits, one brown, one blue, seemingly were swimming in tandem. Their heads were largely in the water, so I couldn't see their faces very well. They swam the Australian crawl in identical style, although one swimmer was gradually gaining a bit on the other. They almost seemed mirror images, even to the white swimming goggles placed in exactly the same position on their heads. I said to Janet "I wonder if they're twins." She said, "Oh no, they're mother and daughter." I peered closely at their faces and was startled to see that one swimmer was much older than the other. In fact, their faces didn't look alike at all. By then, the daughter had overtaken the mother and was halfway down the pool.

Janet didn't think it was strange for a daughter to be just like her mother. To me it is an alien concept. I never really bonded with my mother, as infants are supposed to do. I think the difficulty she had comforting me turned me off from her quite early. It's as if I said, "Well, you can't help me eat, or get me to sleep, or make me less frightened of the world. Why should I pattern myself after you?" I didn't admire my mother's life and didn't want to be like her. I refused to lead what seemed to me a life of household drudgery. Instead I used my teachers, book heroines, and movie stars as models.

I can't help wondering—is this how it's supposed to be, the close relationship between Janet and me? Of course I know that a girl identifies with her mother. According to Freud, identification is the original emotional tie to a love object. In addition, the mother of the little girl is her first model for becoming a woman. But should Janet identify so strongly? I suppose the fact that she "improves" on me for her own purposes answers the question. For example, although we both are to be in private practice, I am interested in pathology, she in maintaining health. Her professional life will be structured as mine was, but even with the inevitable conflicts, she will find herself closer than I to "having it all."

I must admit I am a bit resentful that it is easier for her than it was for me. "It's unfair!" cries the little child within me. When I was growing up, there was no women's movement to give support and encouragement. In my youth I had never met a woman besides my teachers who had a career. No female member of my family had gone beyond high school, and there were only three female relatives who did that. Often ridiculed and minimized for my ambitions, which were seen as unfeminine and rarely taken seriously, I chose a lonely road. I remember one instance in which a well-intentioned neighbor said about my psychoanalytic studies, "After you have your baby, you'll give up all your 'hobbies.' " I'm happy that Janet will be spared such folk wisdom and that her path will be easier in this respect, as is that of many of today's women.

I have some proof from research I did for my doctoral dissertation that a woman who emulates her mother has an easier time in life. The study was called "Grandmothers' Attitudes and Mothers' Concerns." I interviewed 53 pairs of mothers and grandmothers of new babies about their attitudes toward rearing children, surveying them, for example, about harsh or punitive control, overpossessiveness, suppressive attitudes, dislike for homemaking, and demand for striving. Among other things, I tallied how closely the responses of the two generations were similar. The most surprising of the results confirmed my hypothesis that the more the responses of the mothers and grandmothers were alike, the less fearful the mothers were about their newborn babies. It didn't matter whether the replies of the daughters were what generally is considered psychologically "healthy." What counted was only the degree to which the daughters followed in their mothers' footsteps. For example, a mother may have punished her kids harshly, repressed her feelings, and been overpossessive, but if her daughter had similar attitudes, she tended to be less anxious in handling her own babies. If these results are correct, Janet will have a much easier time than I did in raising her child.

My thesis also bears out the adage that the more things change the more they remain the same. I never realized I was interested in grandmothers until now. I thought I picked the topic for my thesis because it was a simple statistical study. There I was at age 33 writing about mothers and grandmothers, when becoming a grandmother was the farthest thing from my mind. The interest was buried in my unconscious, not to emerge again until I was on the brink of becoming a grandparent. Freud was right. There are very few "simple" statistical studies, just as there are few "simple" choices of any kind. Everything we do has meaning, purpose.

♣

September 1

A STRANGE COINCIDENCE: Janet just left a message on my machine. She said she had written an article about my recovery last year from serious injuries in an automobile accident, and the article has been accepted for publication by the magazine, *Modern Maturity*. I'm thrilled for her. She is just beginning her career, and publication will help her. What is uncanny is that I write about her and she writes about me. I guess you might say we are sublimating the distress we feel about our rapidly separating lives. Janet, in this diary, takes the place of her actual presence in my life, just as the Alma of Janet's story makes it unnecessary for her to be actually with her mother. Our sublimations, like our pregnancies, are very much alike.

Mothers and Daughters

53

♣

WHERE DOES IT COME FROM, this universal yearning to be a grandparent? I know about the desire for immortality and the wish to leave something behind when we die. But I feel an urgent, passionate, primitive desire almost as intense as the sex drive. I've always loved babies, peering into every carriage on the street since I was a child. I stopped looking at other babies for a while after I had my own children, but as they reached their teens and developed their own lives, I gradually resumed my peeking into carriages. Now, once again, I gape into them relentlessly.

I got a hint of the origin of this craving while talking to a friend the other day, telling her how my mother had loved being a grandmother. She was so excited at the thought of seeing her new grandchildren that she couldn't sleep the night before they came to visit us in New York from Philadelphia. The day we took the twins home from the hospital, Rudy had to return to his part in *Fiorello,* and it was left to my mother to help out. We left the hospital together, my 68-year-old mother carrying one baby and I, the other. She said later that she'd had the sweet fantasy that people thought the baby I was holding was mine and the one she was carrying was hers.

I remember her rocking one of my newborn twins shortly thereafter. Back and forth, back and forth, she rocked with closed eyes and a smile of rapture on her face. She told me later she had reviewed her whole life as she rocked.

But the most incredible thing she did for a grandchild occurred ten years after her death. Zane, at the height of his adolescence, was a very depressed boy. He was having trouble in school, smoking pot, deserted by his girlfriend. One evening he got in the family car and made for the George Washington Bridge, thinking to drive over the rails of the bridge. As he reached the bridge, the voice of his grandmother came to him. She said, "Zane, you don't want to kill yourself. Turn around and go home."

Although she died when he was only seven years old, Zane knew intuitively that his grandmother loved him. A child's love of his or her mother is ambivalent, contaminated by anger at being disciplined, jealousy of siblings, and rage at the necessary disappointments and frustrations of growing up. The love of a grandparent can be less polluted. Zane's grandmother came to visit, brought presents, cooked his favorite foods, listened to him, and then went home. Not around long enough to disillusion him, an always-loving grandmother is the image he carries. That image saved his life.

As for me, after a lifetime of feeling neglected, it was through my children's grandmother that I was able at last to find *my* mother. We were closest when enjoying them together. I could appreciate her in her new role, and she responded with love. The rapprochement didn't last long enough, however. She died too soon. It is the grandparent in my mother that I miss most of all. The lives of my children surely were impoverished by her death. And for me, some of the joy of being a mother disappeared when my mother was no longer around to enjoy them. She thought nobody on earth was as wonderful. For who can share the narcissism of a parent as well as a grandparent,

Mothers and Daughters

without being restrained by false modesty? I told Janet my feelings about the subject and she said, "I know what you mean. I couldn't stand it if you weren't around to see *my* children."

September 3

MY MOTHER WAS a stolid woman whose experience with my placid, agreeable older sister, Pauline, had been totally gratifying. She expected her second baby (me) to be like the first one. What she got was a difficult, colicky, hyperactive child who screamed around the clock. Mother never knew what to make of me. To her, I was just a "bad baby."

She was uneducated, old-fashioned, and believed mothers should be revered and respected simply because they *were*. It never occurred to her she had to earn my love. I was what would now be diagnosed as a child who suffered from "failure to thrive." Infants with this malady lack age-appropriate signs of social responsiveness and physical development.

When I think about it now, I realize I would have been a difficult child for any woman to raise. I would neither nurse as an infant nor eat as a child. My mother told me she weighed me once before and after nursing me, and I hadn't gained one ounce. Apparently, she either had no milk or there was little nourishment in it, and I cried at least in part because I was hungry. In the era when fat babies were a sign of successful mothering, I weighed only 21 pounds at the age of three, announcing to all the world her "failure" as a mother.

On Becoming a Grandparent
56

If she had simply continued to show she loved me without retaliating with hostility, I eventually would have come around and accepted her as a devoted mother. I learned that from my experience with my son Jonny, who took two years to openly show his love for me. But how was the simple, psychologically untutored woman who was my mother to know that, sooner or later, her persistence would have paid off?

She was not the most secure of individuals. "Did Mrs. Holtz go to high school?" my mother, who had gone only to the fourth grade in Romania, would wistfully inquire. Or, "Am I fatter than Mrs. Glauser?" she, who was sensitive about her "zaftig" build, would ask. My continuous crying and inability to gain weight did not add to my mother's feelings of adequacy.

Helpless in her efforts to comfort me, her label of "bad baby" stuck to me throughout my growing-up years. "You bad child, you!" she would shriek in despair when I refused to put down my book immediately to go wash the dishes. "Ugly face! Bad, bad, bad!" Frustrated to the breaking point, she didn't know that if she had said, "Please, dear, I need your help," I would have run gladly to her side.

Eventually my parents hired a woman named Victoria to take care of me when I was a baby. She rocked me night and day, singing the quintessential song of symbiosis, "You and me, me and you," over and over again. As long as she rocked, I was quiet. I was a miserable, hungry infant, and apparently Victoria's warm body and symbiotic song comforted me temporarily.

Once when I was deeply distressed, an encapsulated

memory, an engram almost in the form of a hallucination, came back to me with overwhelming urgency. Back and forth, back and forth my body moved. The uncontrollable movement terrified me until I understood what it was. In an unconscious fantasy at the age of 40, I was rocking with Victoria, returning to the solace she had given me as an infant.

I decided to seek out Victoria, and told an analyst friend about it. She responded, "What would you do if you found her?" I said, "Of course," and dropped the idea. By then, I was a bit old to be rocked.

Victoria's song, "You and me, me and you," and the reassuring bodily warmth I was able to accept so readily reminds me of the work of Margaret Mahler on symbiosis and separation-individuation. According to Mahler, young children pass through a number of stages on their way to developing selfhood. She says that the newborn and mother live in a state of almost complete symbiotic union, reproducing insofar as possible the absolute fusion of pregnant woman and fetus. It is out of this matrix of oneness that the infant emerges into selfhood. When he or she cannot enter into and grow out of this phase, whether because of constitutional impairment or some deficiency in the mothering process, psychological development cannot proceed normally.

Why did I fail to bond with my mother, who was what George Winocott called a "good-enough mother" to my brother and sister? Many people who experienced far worse mothering are able to forgive their mothers and proceed normally with their development. It is possible to speculate endlessly on this question. Oddly enough, a revelation came to me while I was doing research for this diary.

I was reading Thomas Verny's *The Secret Life of the Unborn Child*, in which the author recounts a case called "Kristine," as told to him by Dr. Peter Fedor-Freyburgh. The child described sounded so much like me as an infant that I literally became dizzy. Kristine was a robust and healthy child at birth. (And I was told that I was a well-formed, seven-pound infant.) Unlike bonding babies, however, who invariably move toward the maternal breast, Kristine turned away from her mother. But when placed in the vicinity of another nursing mother, Kristine grasped her nipple and began to suck vigorously at it.

When asked if she had wanted to get pregnant, Kristine's mother confessed that she had not wanted a child and wished to have an abortion. She continued the pregnancy only at the insistence of her husband.

Dr. Fedor-Freyburgh concluded that Kristine had been painfully aware of her mother's rejection for a long time, and refused to bond with her mother after birth because the woman had refused to fuse with the embryo before she was born. "Kristine had been shut out emotionally in the womb," the doctor continued, "and now, though only four days old, she was determined to protect herself from her mother."

There were seven years between my birth and my sister's. My mother wasn't in any hurry to have a second child. I am convinced that I, like Kristine, was an unwanted child. One of my greatest skills as an analyst is the ability to recognize hostility. I'm always aware when a patient doesn't like me. Perhaps I learned this skill at the beginning of my existence. How dreadful to be forced to depend for the very breath of life on someone who doesn't want you! Surely not many emotions are as painful. Like Kristine, I learned early to protect myself from the anguish.

When Mother turned me over to Victoria, she taught me that the solution to our dilemma lay with another person. And didn't I take the same path in adulthood, when I improved so rapidly under the tutelage of a warm woman analyst, Dr. B? And come to think of it, isn't that what I've been doing my whole psychoanalytic career, playing Victoria to appease the yearnings of some grown-up infant?

♣

September 3 (later)

ANOTHER EXPERIENCE CONFIRMED my belief that the rupture of a symbiosis can, at least sometimes, be healed relatively easily in early childhood if another person is willing to lend herself (or himself) to the symbiotic experience. I learned this from Hilary, an 18-month-old child I saw four times at Masters' Children's Center, where I assisted Margaret Mahler in her pioneering research on separation-individuation.

At the time of our first encounter, Hilary was notorious at the center for being unresponsive to female staff members. She seemed not to hear if one spoke to her. If approached by a woman, she "looked right through her" or ran away. Worst of all, like me, Hilary ignored her mother. One of the staff commented, "Mrs. S a couple of times has made remarks about how Hilary never notices her, and I often have the feeling she feels rejected by this." As a result, Mrs. S would follow her daughter around, as if entreating her to pay attention, but the child continued to slight her or dart away. Though the other children generally seemed to enjoy their mothers, Hilary spent her time at the nursery lying before a mirror watching herself rock back and forth.

The first time we met, I was talking quietly with another staff member. Hilary approached me, stopped, and dropped a semicircular hand over each eye. Then she retreated. Several moments later, she advanced again, using the same hand motion. Then in one quick motion, she grabbed a large white plate, thrust it at me, and darted away. I wondered if the attempt at intimacy was too much for her to tolerate.

For the next 20 minutes or so she ostensibly ignored me, but I felt that much of her activity was a substitute for mothering. For example, she seemed to experience a sensual pleasure in rubbing the full length of her body against the large flat table top.

Then she again approached me directly. This time she handed me a top. "Thank you," I said with obvious pleasure, the two of us in an eye lock. Then, abruptly, she turned to the playpen and picked up a large cuddly bear. She hugged it to her lovingly, swaying gently from side to side, murmuring, "Bear . . . bear . . . bear." "Yes, bear," I said, as we looked into each other's eyes.

It was a month later when we met again. She came into the playroom and moved fairly close to me. I held out a little plastic doll I had bought for her. She came closer joyfully, but did not reach out for the doll. I waited, still holding out the doll. It took only a moment until she grabbed it, chortling sounds of rapture.

Hilary's behavior then changed to what is best characterized as the "whither thou goest" syndrome. If she went to the sink, she knew I would follow. For perhaps 30 or 40 minutes she clearly communicated what she wanted and felt by grunts, pointing, monosyllables, and whatever. I had a strong feeling that this 18-month-old child and I were really conversing, although few words were spoken.

Two weeks later, her mother was away, and I went to visit Hilary at home. When she first saw me, she quickly curled her fingers over her eyes, as she had done at our first meeting. Then suddenly she opened wide her fingers, peeked out at me, and burst into gales of laughter. I put my hands over my eyes, peeked out at her, and began to laugh too. We laughed and laughed together. An autistic mannerism had departed and left instead a delightful child mastering her anxiety normally.

There followed an interval in which she excitedly dashed back and forth, showing me all her treasures. Then she ran to the door and urgently said, "Mama. Car. Gone," with better speech than I had ever heard her use before. After that she came to me and handed me her favorite doll. Soon she seized it back, and hastily climbed into my lap.

I saw Hilary only once after that. I had heard that a striking change had occurred in her interaction with other staff members, and in particular, with her mother. Reports were that the child now persistently exuded a longing for her mother, followed her about, yearned for her when away, cried for her, and seemed to delight in her company. A brief contact with Hilary confirmed this.

Hilary passed me in the hall. She was crying for her mother. "Mama, mama, mama," wept this child, whose vocabulary had not even included a word for mother until after our first meeting. "Mama, mama," she entreated me plaintively. I took her by the hand and said, "Let's go find Mommy."

Eight years later, I met Mrs. S at a party. She did not recognize me. I told her we had met a long time before at Masters' Children Center, and asked how Hilary was. "She's wonderful," the mother answered. "In fact, emotionally speaking, she's the healthiest one in the family."

Hilary seems to have picked up her development where it left off. She did not have to wait until she was a grandmother to repair a broken symbiosis.

♣

September 4

WHILE I FOUND SHADES of my infant self in Hilary, longing, forever searching for a mother, I experienced the mother side of the coin in my relationship with Selena S———. A 30-year-old patient, Selena had been rejected as an infant by *her* mother. I learned that her mother had left the infant Selena alone in her crib for endless hours. Selena had apparently responded by turning her back on her mother and the world. Much of our analysis was a reenactment of those early years. Selena was the sick baby, casting me as the rejecting mother. She lay hour after hour with her face to the wall, having fantasies that she was dying. In that state, there was no interpretation she was

Mothers and Daughters

able to accept. My words were like milk to an infant who refuses the breast.

Much to my despair, this 30-year-old baby wouldn't "swallow" the mothering of an analyst, and I was really afraid for her life. Her rejection of everything, including me, was excruciatingly painful. The prominent analyst to whom I went for consultation on the case said, "Get rid of her and get a better patient." I found myself just sitting with Selena for months, until gradually she was able to understand that she was reenacting the past. She eventually recovered.

But the sessions were so painful that I found myself writing a poem to help me. I called it "The Deathbed Watch," and part of it went:

> *How to stay*
> *The sorrowful sigh*
> *When the infant*
> *Determines to die.*

I realized that through empathy with Selena, I myself had reexperienced the despair I had suffered as an infant. By working with my patient, I was also able to encounter the pain I had involuntarily inflicted on my mother, adding to her already great feelings of inadequacy. With Selena, I learned that by denying my love, I injured both my mother and myself.

♣

September 5

GROWING UP WITHOUT a role model is very difficult. The paths other children take for granted have to be negotiated every step of the way. Transitions are particularly painful and frightening, when one has to make them alone. Perhaps this is why they still are so difficult for me, even now, when I'm in the process of becoming a grandmother. I had no one to guide me through the terrors of nighttime, the anguish of adolescence, the ordeal of becoming independent.

I remember clearly my contempt for my mother. Since she hadn't been able to perform the simplest task of motherhood, that of making her infant comfortable, I had no use for her for many years. Instead I grew up in a fantasy world in which my *real* mother was not incompetent; she was a woman who had the answers to everything. Like Barbara Stanwyck.

It's laughable now, but it was so important to me then, as an impressionable teenager. At first I wondered why I chose Stanwyck, since her acting roles (and I never missed one) generally cast her not as a nurturer, but as a tough, independent female. But years later at an awards ceremony, I heard a young starlet speak of her. She called Stanwyck "Missy" and said Stanwyck had been her mentor and like a mother to her. She ended her talk with, "I love you, Missy." Of course, that could have been Hollywood baloney, but I remember being pleased that the woman I had picked to be my fantasy mother turned out to be okay after all. So, with help from books and the movies, I essentially raised myself. But the search for a mother precipitated a lifetime of psychoanalysis and self-analysis.

A patient of mine with a similar emotional history had a dream in which she was trying to walk up a stairway, but the steps seemed appallingly far apart, and she had to strain and stretch to reach the next one. That was the way she had felt as a child, that each step to emotional maturity was ominous without the ministrations of a concerned and loving parent.

Perhaps that is why my relationships with my children are more important to me than they are for most people. Rejection by my children would be even more devastating than parental rejection. I have almost always been nourished by them, as I wasn't by my mother.

☙

September 5 (later)

ON REREADING THE ANECDOTE in which my mother and I are each carrying a baby out of the hospital, I note a discrepancy. Did the fantasy that one baby was mine and one my mother's originate with my mother, as I said? Now I think the fantasy was mine.

At the time, although I didn't know it, my mother had only a few more months to live. I can see her clearly, walking behind me out of the hospital, slowly, heavily, stooped and gnarled with arthritis. Grateful for her help but worried that she would drop the baby, I pictured her as a woman who was coming to the end of her life, while I was at the prime of mine. I think I decided then to make us equals—she the mother of one infant, I the other. My guilt at having to ask her for help could be assuaged in this way, and we could have "our" babies together.

Freud would have liked my solution. It was like his case study of Little Hans. At the end of his analysis, the five-year-old boy found an ingenious solution to his

Oedipus complex that enabled him to avoid guilt and anxiety about his father. He had a fantasy that he took his mother for himself, awarding to his father *his* mother.

So, even if my mother and I were a totally mismatched couple for so long, I found a way to bond with her before she died. She shone as a grandmother; in fact, she laid down the blueprint for grandparenting. Because of her, I think my new role will come easily to me. Because of her, I know how to be a grandmother without ever having experienced it. Because of my mother, this time I don't have to be a pioneer. I must have been cruel as an infant and child, disguising nothing. Later on, I learned to temper my responses, to protect the feelings of those I loved. For the infant, there are no subterfuges; there is only the immediate world of pleasure and pain.

And I have written another poem:

> *Flat feet size seven D*
> *disjointed with corns and bunions*
> *who was there to tell her*
> *that pinioned inside were*
> *dainty silk-shod tiny toes?*

♣

September 12

My friend, writer and psychologist Arlene Richards, has just returned from a visit with her new grandson. She showed me Polaroid shots of her sticking her tongue out at the infant, and the infant responding in the same way. Arlene had discovered that even new babies imitate adults, and documented her theory with her own photographs.

Investigators have confirmed that, as Richards maintains, the newborn is a very talented mimic. Many skills must be mastered to develop this ability. For example, the child has to understand that the adult wants to be imitated. Then he or she has to learn to copy the gesture. And then the infant must be enticed into the game by the pleasure experienced by the person being copied. Apparently even new-born infants are capable of mimicking. In a landmark study done in 1977, Meltzoff and Moore had a nursery full of babies imitating them. Some of these babies were only one hour old. When a researcher stuck out his or her tongue, made a face, or wiggled fingers in front of a baby, the child often responded in kind. A more recent study of 74 newborns revealed that they could recognize and imitate expressions of surprise, happiness, and sadness.

I can hardly wait to see the first evidence of my grandchild's mind. So I got out my old Polaroid and dusted it off.

♣

September 15

I'M FEELING SO HAPPY these days, perhaps the happiest of my entire life. I like my "rapprochement" theory, that being a grandparent helps us reconnect on many levels with our lost loved ones.

It also replicates the bliss of being in love. Several grandparents have told me that they are happier being grandparents than they were as parents. For example, my daughter's mother-in-law, a happily married woman who cherishes her children, says she loves her one grandchild better. I believe that my love and yearning for my grandchild is purer, less contaminated by the exigencies of everyday life. Without the terrible burdens of childrearing, I can afford to concentrate on loving. Freud said a mother's love for her son is the purest love that exists. In this instance, I think he was wrong.

Just today a patient bore this out. Marjorie, a 60-year-old psychotherapist, came into treatment six months ago because she was depressed that she and her daughter Elsa were estranged. Elsa has since had a baby, and in the past few months the two have become reconciled. Marjorie brought in this dream: "I am on a bus going home. There is a baby on the bus. I think the baby is me. Or maybe it looks like Elsa when she was about ten months old. I get off the bus and all of a sudden—just like that—I left the baby—she just disappeared. I also had forgotten my suitcase, and went back to the bus to try to find it. The bus driver tells me that the suitcase will come in on the ten o'clock bus."

Marjorie explained, "Ten o'clock makes me think of an appointment I had at ten o'clock with a sad and lonely man who is in therapy. Like me. Going home makes me think of my analysis. That's what I am doing here, going back."

I said, "Yes, you are going back to the time you and Elsa were happiest together—when she was ten months old. You are also returning to the time when you were a baby, when you and your mother delighted in each other's company. You said that after you started to walk, she lost interest in you.

Mothers and Daughters

"So being a grandmother means a rapprochement—with your daughter, with the baby in both of you, and with the mother of your infancy," I said. "That's why you feel so good."

"Right," she solemnly added. "And that's why I needed desperately for Elsa to let me be a good grand-mother . . . Since we got together again, I've never been happier."

And I thought, in harmony, "Just like me."

CHAPTER

V

My Grandmothers

September 17

RAPPROCHEMENT WITH MY MOTHER takes me even further back, to my grandmothers, who, I now realize, were influential to an extraordinary degree in my life.

My mother's mother was considered a lady, very beautiful, with a reputation for being haughty. It was rumored that her family, the Weisses, was neither affectionate nor open with their feelings. I know from my own experience that people can appear cold without being so, just reluctant to reveal what is going on inside them. Did the Weisses love my mother and her children? Were they shy? Or were they really unfeeling, as whispered by my mother's in-laws? I never knew. I simply believed my grandmother was a queen.

She and my grandfather, who had been the owner of a small department store in Romania, came to this country sometime around 1910. What I remember most vividly about her is that all 7 children, their mates, and the

My Grandmothers

71

15 grandchildren would go visit every Sunday and pay homage as if she were royalty. "Let's go visit Mutter today," my mother would say each Sunday, as if she had never thought of it before. (It is interesting that she never said, "Let's go visit 'Fater.' ") All of us would congregate in the cramped living room of my grandparent's small Philadelphia row house, and I marveled that the crowded room held 29 people who had come from one set of parents.

My grandmother was always gracious and welcoming, serving us a teaspoon of homemade blackberry jam floating on top of a glass of seltzer. She enjoyed being loved and courted, but I don't remember that she ever reacted with ardor to any of her grandchildren. She reigned, instead.

Elegant as she was, Mutter always seemed very old. I am startled to realize that when I was born she was in her fifties, much younger than I am now. She already had white hair gathered in a loose bun at the back of her head, a version of the hairdo worn by Wallis Warfield, the duchess of Windsor. I have always loved that hairstyle; when I sculpted the head of a woman a few years back, that's the hairstyle I gave her. A friend read some of this diary and wrote on this page, "Didn't Virginia Woolf wear her hair in that style?" She is right; my grandmother's hairstyle was exactly like Virginia Woolf's in a favorite portrait of her. I wouldn't be surprised if V. W.'s coiffure and queenly bearing were part of the reason I wrote *Who Killed Virginia Woolf?* and entered into a seven-year-long obsession with the writer.

When I think of my mother and grandmother, I am surprised to realize the differences between them. Grandmother was gracious and queenly. Mother, short and stocky, looked like a peasant. Grandmother had beautiful, classic features; mother had a square face and wore large, round glasses. It must have been very difficult for her to have such a beautiful mother. I'm afraid I took my mother's opinion of herself at face value, and loved and admired Mutter more.

Mutter weighed 120 pounds practically all her life. So, to me, 120 pounds is an ideal weight, the cutoff point below which I don't feel fat.

After my grandfather died at age 90, my grandmother, who was a few years younger, developed diabetes. Gangrene set in and cost her a big toe. After she recovered somewhat, the hospital called and said she couldn't stay there any longer, that the children would have to come get her. None of her "adoring" children except my mother was willing to take her into their home. My regal grandmother was relegated to a bed in our downstairs dining room. When caring got to be too much for my mother, my proud grandmother was sent to a nursing home. I went to pay her a visit. We didn't speak of love or family mistakes or illness, but sat there quietly together. Finally, after a long pause, Grandmother said to her renegade granddaughter who hadn't the slightest interest in clothing, "Have you bought any new dresses lately?"

Like her husband, Grandmother died at age 90, on February 8, 1948. I got married on February 1 of that year, and my cousin Nancy's wedding was on February 15. According to Freud, all people wish to die in their own fashion, to follow their own circuitous path to death. I believe this explains why so many people die only after a special birthday, or an event they wish to honor. My grandmother's death confirmed this idea for me. Didn't she die on the Sunday between her two granddaughters' weddings, scheduling her death so as not to ruin our pleasure?

I only knew my maternal grandmother, but in some sense my paternal grandmother, who died in Poland when my father was still a young man, had an even greater effect on my life.

She lived during the latter part of the nineteenth century in a repressive Polish society, when women were denied all meaningful political and cultural life. Although a women's movement, as we know it, still has not emerged in Poland, more than 100 years ago Grandmother believed that women should be permitted to have careers if they chose, and to experience the same independence as men. She was one of those women who rebelled against the prevailing ideology of the times by overthrowing all ties of obedience to their husband.

The Jewish proletariat of the time opposed the employment of mothers and worked to counteract such independence, forcing women in Poland to give up work after marriage, and particularly after having borne a child. But Grandmother made a career for herself in my grandfather's tobacco company.

No doubt encouraged by her professional success, my grandmother developed an unusual habit for a woman in those days: she smoked. Somewhere around 1890, when my father was three years old, his mother further demonstrated her penchant for independent action: she decided she didn't want to live any longer with her husband and left him to raise their three children by himself, again a very unusual action for a Polish woman of her time.

Several years later she died of stomach cancer. Many people today would no doubt attribute the death of my grandmother to her fondness for tobacco, but in my opinion the mind and body cannot be separated, or as Dr. George Solomon said, "The mind is the brain and the brain is part of the body. The brain regulates and influences many physiological functions, including immunity. Mental and physical well-being are inextricably intertwined."

Research such as Solomon's suggests that cancer often occurs in people who have experienced some deep trauma in life. Did my grandmother find the traditional patriarchal structure of the times unbearable? Was her husband brutal or asexual, overly demanding or critical? Did she fall in love and run away with another man? I'll never understand her troubles, just as I'll never know why she felt she couldn't live with her husband. But I can imagine the pain her defection caused her abandoned son, my father, and I can understand the aberrations in his personality that resulted, such as his occasional outbursts of rage.

Despite his loss, my father had the courage at age 13 to leave Poland and come to this country alone, thereby avoiding the pogroms and acts of violence against the Jews. His strength enabled him to overcome early deprivation and become successful in business.

In contrast to my mother, who often was depressed

and unavailable, my father was mostly warmhearted and tender. I often felt he understood me when nobody else did.

I never knew a person who didn't like him. Once he told me he would "sell his shirt" to send me to college. But his amiability must have been purchased at a terrible cost, for rage lay just beneath the surface, fury brought on, no doubt, by his abandonment by his mother. In many ways he was immature, volatile, and erratic; his temper could be terrifying at times. But I realize now that he hadn't the slightest idea about raising children. How could he?

For example, he believed that children should "behave" at all costs. I was never exactly sure what "behaving" meant. Some days, minor infractions like refusing to eat spinach quickly brought out the belt strap. On other days, major transgressions were ignored.

I remember a particularly debilitating incident on my twelfth birthday. On the way home from school, I passed a store window with a pair of shoes, shiny brown oxfords with a Scottish "tongue" over the laces. But most intriguing of all to a 12-year-old, they had initials on the tongue. At an age when adolescents are struggling for an identity, I thought it would be wonderful to have shoes with an *A* for Alma on them. The store owner said he would bring them to my house that evening and see if my parents and I liked them. I agreed.

But when the man came to the house, despite the *A* on the front of the desirable shoes, I now thought they looked too masculine. So I said that I had changed my mind. Another parent might have been annoyed at a child's fickleness and the resultant inconvenience to all. But my father, apparently humiliated in front of the store owner, sent the man away, then proceeded to give me the worst whipping of my life. Immediately after, apparently stricken with guilt, he raised my allowance.

My father always spoke of his mother with love and admiration. I don't remember a critical word about the abandonment. I don't believe he was even aware he was angry with her or knew why his rage was always so ready to break out. Sometimes, I think my father never really understood the difference between his mother and his daughter. In his unconscious mind, we were entwined as closely as roses and thorns. According to legend, she was a wise woman to whom people came from miles around for guidance. When I became a psychoanalyst, I felt I had a role model in my dead grandmother, to whom "even lawyers came for advice." (How thrilled I was when I worked with my first lawyer patient.) It is only as I write this that I realize I shared my father's idealization of his mother. Never once did I question her abandonment of her three-year-old son.

It's been a rewarding experience, writing about my grandmothers. These memories of my own development give me better access to my relationship with my children and grandchildren-to-be. Reliving old memories adds a richer dimension to my life, as I more fully understand the complicated dynamics of my family.

I see that in contrast to my mother, about whom I felt ambivalence at best, both my grandmothers were revered and adored by their children. All of us tend to identify with our heroes and heroines. I never wanted to be like my mother but like the "bubbas," instead. No wonder I can hardly wait to be a grandmother. I want to be a heroine, too.

VI

Six Weeks to Go

September 18

MY FIRST GRANDCHILD in the womb is 34 weeks old today. The infant's chances of survival would be approximately 95 percent if the birth occurred now. I read these statistics carefully, and find the survival rate reassuring. At full term, a fetus's chances of being born alive are 99 percent. But the best reassurance will be holding the baby in my arms.

I am doing more research. I find that the fine soft woolly down that grows over the body of the unborn child is almost gone by now. The hair on his or her head, eyebrows, and eyelashes is slowly growing in. "My" baby's hair at this stage is just short enough to look nicely trimmed, as though he or she has recently been given a haircut. About a month ago, secretions from the sebaceous glands began to form a kind of skin ointment, protecting the fetus from skin infections. So I'm afraid s/he looks a bit greasy right now, and will remain so until washed off after birth. That's all right, baby. Perhaps you'll grow up to be a garage mechanic.

Fingernails are coming in nicely, too, at this time. In one picture I saw of a fetus around this age, its fingers had dug a groove on its forehead. I don't know how this happened, but the sonogram showed a deep ridge. Make a fist, little one. I don't want you hurt before you are even born. But wait! There's nothing to worry about. We are told there is no chance of scratches; the nails are reassuringly short.

My baby can now suck his thumb, and grasp her own umbilical cord. As Janet knows well, s/he can also kick his legs and wave her arms. New discoveries tell us that the baby can hear his mother's voice, the pounding of her pulse, and the placenta's surges and murmurs. In fact, recent research suggests that after the twenty-fourth week the unborn child is "all ears"; it listens all the time. A fetus has no muffling air cushions around its eardrum, to correspond with eyelids that protect its eyes. And water conducts sound better than air.

So the silent world of the womb is a myth. This baby already is a little human being who is very interested in the world outside and even exhibits distinct musical likes and dislikes.

Wendy later confirmed this. She said her unborn baby kicked so hard during the musical *Les Miserables* that she had to leave the theater. Does that mean that after the birth we won't have to be quiet so the baby can sleep? In utero, s/he has already sampled our ultranoisy world.

I have another worry, a little "disquietude." The books say Janet's baby should be kicking vigorously and continuously by now. The baby is relatively quiet and kicked only a few times the other day when I was with her. Could anything be wrong? When I carried the twins, it seemed to me that one child kicked vigorously while the other seemed much less active. I decided that Jonny was the kicker and Janet the one in repose, for he became a hyperactive child, while she was gentle and contented. I pray that the relative quiescence of this baby means merely that he or she has inherited its mother's disposition.

There are approximately six weeks left to delivery. The fetus is now very close to the uterine wall. The womb is getting quite crowded, and the baby has grown so large that there is no room to turn around. The child could be feeling claustrophobic and ready to leave its studio apartment.

♣

September 19

I TALKED TO JANET tonight, and my anxieties about the baby's position and movement are allayed. She went to the doctor today, and all is well. The baby's head has turned and has settled quite deeply into her pelvis. There will be no breech for her.

"Then," she said, her voice trilling with delight, "the doctor said 'Feel this little bump up here? Well, that's the baby's foot.' Now I keep touching it every time the baby kicks. It's like a little knob. I know it's the foot because it's too far away from the head to be the hand." So much for my foolish fears.

Six Weeks to Go

September 20

WENDY IS STILL PREGNANT, thank goodness. She stained a little at about six weeks, and we all worried about her. But she's been in good shape since, and will hit the three-month mark any day now. She has expanded a bit in the waistline already. Since Wendy, her parents, Jonny, and I all have dark coloring and even features, it is likely her baby will resemble us. Of course, there is no guarantee. S/he could turn out to look like Groucho Marx!

Although Wendy was still ambivalent about the pregnancy when I saw her last, she has settled down and is now very happy. I told her everyone has mixed feelings about having children, but not everyone is honest enough to say so.

✿

September 22

DREAMS ARE ONE of the most beneficial means pregnant women have to deal with their anxiety. Dr. Ernest Hartmann, director of the Sleep Disorders Center at Newton-Wellesley Hospital in Massachussetts, found that women dream more when hormone levels are high, most notably during pregnancy. This is a good thing, because it turns out that expectant mothers who have anxiety dreams tend to have shorter labors and easier births.

Self magazine reports that pregnant women may work out their psychological conflicts about pregnancy through strange and frightening dreams. Dr. Patricia

Maybruck examined the dreams of 67 pregnant women and discovered that 40 percent of the dreams were nightmares. The dreams frequently dealt with such themes as fires, floods, and disasters, and signaled the women's fears that something might go wrong with their pregnancies. Janet sent me a few dreams recently that I haven't had a chance to read yet. Think I'll look them over and check out Maybruck's theory.

Janet, like Wendy and Sam, has also dreamed of twins—both girls in her case. I know she would prefer girls. When Rudy and I first found out we were having twins and thought they might be identical, Rudy, already the father of Zane, said he'd take two girls if need be, preferring *two* girls to *no* girls.

In Janet's dream, one baby is healthy and one small and sickly. Janet was strong at birth, but Jonny was puny. The nurse told me that if he lost a few pounds, he might not survive. I wonder if Janet is afraid her baby will have the same poor start her brother had. In my interpretation, a part of her feels too small and incompetent for what will be demanded of her, in contrast to the capable woman she really is.

In the second part of her dream, the baby is bottle fed "by mistake." Janet gets upset that she isn't breast-feeding the baby and demands to do so. The nurses say it is too late, that "once you start you can't switch." Janet then replies, "No, you're wrong, let me see the doctor about it."

I think this part of the dream represents the unconscious conflict she must have about breast-feeding, and her determination to resolve it. I didn't nurse my children,

Six Weeks to Go

which I regret. First of all, I think I missed an exquisite experience, although my children seemed to enjoy being fed, as they were always held and cuddled when we gave them a bottle. Second, Janet asked me about it and said she feels deprived at not having been nursed. I believe it was my own conflict about breast-feeding, uncovered in psychoanalysis later, that was responsible—a conflict that unfortunately might have been passed on to my daughter. Mine, I'm sure, originated in the disastrous experience I had when my mother breast-fed me. If I had it to do over again, I would nurse my children.

The last part of Janet's dream deals with names for the baby. She feels the child's first name must begin with the letter *R*, in memory of her father, Rudy. But another part of her wishes to name the child after me, and she probably will try to do so with the baby's middle name. Since Hebrew law does not permit naming a baby after a living person, she cannot use "Alma" but is thinking of names beginning with an *A*, which would be in my honor. In the dream she says, "I said to everyone how happy I was that there were two babies because now I could use the *R* with one of them and still have another baby to name any name I wanted." Having twins would satisfy both her conscience and her wishes.

In my opinion Janet, like all new mothers, has many concerns about her child. She is worried about its sex and birth weight, her competence to care for it—particularly whether she can breast-feed or not—and if she can name her child what she pleases. The dream is a success: it resolves all her problems. By having twins, she gets the girl she wants and has at least one healthy child. In addition,

On Becoming a Grandparent

she settles both the breast-feeding conflict and her struggle over names. If only we could all resolve our nighttime terrors as easily.

♣

JANET TALKS to her baby. She talks gently, sweetly, tentatively, as if she is introducing herself to her child, and her child to her. She reminds me of the Vietnamese mother-to-be in the story "Mid-Autumn," by Robert Olen Butler. The woman tells her baby that although it isn't the custom among Americans, the Vietnamese talk to their unborn babies, to counsel them in the ways of the world. She says to the baby that her own mother spoke to her in the womb, and sometimes when she dreams and wakes and cannot remember, the feeling is of her mother's voice plunging like a swimmer into the sea and swimming strongly to her, where she is waiting deep beneath the waves. I hope Janet's baby, too, will remember the otherworldly sound of her mother's voice and its sweetness.

Sam talks to his baby, too. Janet sent me the following note yesterday, "Since the baby has started kicking and Sam has been able to feel it, he plays a game with it. He talks to it saying 'Hi baby, hi baby . . .' Then he waits for it to kick. Usually it does, and he's convinced that the baby senses him and is responding." He is more progressive than the modernists who advocate equal participation of fathers and mothers in childrearing. I don't think even they have recommended that the father begin a relationship with his child in the womb.

❦

SAM'S MOTHER AND I have had a tiff over the baby. I visited Sam and Janet in Florida last weekend for Janet's thirtieth birthday. When I asked what birthday present she would like, she said, "The layette." So we went shopping and ordered a carriage, a Snugli, Carters baby kimonos and various sheets, diapers, booties, and so on, all to be picked up after the baby is born. It was great fun to choose things for the baby. It made the whole idea of the grandchild even more real. I had bought a lot of the same items, including Carters kimonos, for my own children. My mother and I had selected my first baby's layette together, and Janet and I had been looking forward to doing the same thing. I left the shop immersed in good feelings about Janet, her baby, my mother and myself.

That evening her generous in-laws gave a dinner party for Janet and presented her with a beautiful silver necklace with five small diamonds in it. Janet opened her other birthday presents, too, and everybody seemed very happy until she informed the group what I had given her for her birthday. Then her mother-in-law, Edna, announced in front of the guests: "You should have left something for me to give."

I tried to ignore the remark. Then I decided I had to speak up or I would be upset for a long time. When the party was over I went up to Edna and said: "Please don't tell me what I can give my daughter. And Janet still needs many things, for example a car seat."

"Oh, a car seat," she answered contemptuously.

I found it hard to sleep that night, but the next morning Edna called, not holding a grudge. We talked about the birthday as if nothing had happened between us.

Later Janet and I discussed the incident with several of her friends. Janet said, "Maybe I should have invited her to shop with us, but that's the kind of thing you want to do with your own mother." I felt a bit vindicated, but I still regret the whole episode. Edna has two sons, and has always wanted a daughter. She thinks of Janet as her own child. It would have been generous to have invited her along for the shopping expedition.

❧

September 30

A PATIENT OF MINE who has adopted a newborn brought him to her analytic hour yesterday. He weighs five pounds and is about the size of my hand. He has a beautifully shaped head, straight black hair, and sleeps the 23 and a half hours a day infants are supposed to but usually don't. The mother goes about her business as if she simply has picked up another passenger on the highway of her life.

She entered the office, put the baby down on the couch, and, taking the chair opposite me, proceeded with her hour. The baby slept. Suddenly, a miracle! Out of the dimness of the newborn's world, the baby awoke. His eyes swept the room. Finding his mother, he stared at her for a long moment with his huge black eyes. Then he went back to sleep.

At the end of the hour I picked him up. Once again, that magical sense of awareness. He somehow understood that I wasn't his mother. He doesn't know yet how to reach out with his arms, but his whole five pounds frantically strained toward her. According to researcher C. Trevarthen, infants thrust their body at their mother quite early.

I felt I had witnessed the birth of consciousness. It began with the baby's anxiety that he and his mother were apart. It lasted until he satisfied himself that she was nearby. Then he could return to blissful sleep.

In almost 40 years of practice, I have learned that this is the way it will be for the rest of his life. If the child is in touch with the "good mother" outside or inside himself, he will be able to sleep. When he loses her, literally or emotionally, he will be wakeful. Consciously or otherwise, whatever his age, he'll long to return to his mother. Some attempt to substitute cigarettes or drugs for mother; others try to emulate her and, by gratifying others, vicariously satisfy themselves. The lucky ones find a mother in their mate. The result is a normally functioning human being, at peace with himself.

VII

The Long Wait

October 24

TEN DAYS TO GO! I couldn't sleep last night. Yesterday a patient who often is clairvoyant said she had a feeling the baby would be born this week. I was so convinced I'd get a midnight phone call that Janet's labor had begun, I got up and packed. But it was a false alarm.

Janet has asked me to come to Florida when the baby is born, so I've alerted all my patients that I will be called away. I'm not making any extra appointments for the next few weeks that I may have to cancel. Of course the baby may be late, in which case I'll be sitting around for nothing.

My children all took their time arriving, and Janet is carrying almost exactly the way I did. Zane was actually three weeks off schedule. He had the umbilical cord wrapped around his neck and I suppose every time he tried to turn it choked him. So he wasn't in any hurry to emerge. That probably explains why he isn't in any rush to get places on time today. I understand doctors no longer allow such difficult natural births, but instead deliver the child by Caesarean.

Janet and Johnny were one week late, even though they were twins, which are usually born prematurely. The delay was good, because twins often have a low birth weight and the extra time gave them a better start. Somewhere in my reading, I came across the information that women tend to have births similar to the kind their mothers had, so we might suppose that Janet will be late, too. If this theory is correct, we also should be able to predict the approximate date of birth of Wendy and Jonny's infant. Her mother delivered Wendy, her first child, three weeks early. So, hypothetically, we can expect the youngest Bond baby around February 11.

When I recounted the story about "Daddy, Daddy, it's a real one," I said that my father had promised me a new baby for Christmas. But my brother didn't arrive until January 6. So my mother's third child was 12 days late. Now I recall she jokingly said that she had carried me for ten months. So I guess it could be true that daughters generally carry the way their mothers did. I lived through my long wait, as my mother did before me. I will try to be calm this time around, too.

I try not to contemplate the problems that could come up for Janet or the baby in childbirth. Janet told me over the phone last night about a child she saw on television who was born without a brain. She said it had only a face, with a flat back where the head should be. Its heart was used as a transplant for another baby born with a malformed heart. It's almost a miracle when a child is born healthy and whole.

So many possibilities for disaster: Down syndrome, spina bifida, cleft palate, dwarfism, clubfoot, cerebral palsy, disfiguring birthmarks, RH negative blood and hemolytic disease, blindness, deafness, and blue babies, for starters. Not to mention malfunctioning heart, lungs, or liver. Well, Janet's baby's head looks fine in the sonogram, with two arms, two legs, and a closed spine. Whether all else is well, only time will tell.

Janet said, "Sam isn't sleeping, either. He keeps jumping up, walking around, and turning on the television."

"How about you?" I asked.

"Oh, I'm fine," she answered. "I sleep soundly— until he wakes me up."

I'm proud of my daughter. She has faced her fears about childbirth and hopefully put them to rest.

♣

October 25

NOW I'M THE ONE having nightmares. I am out walking in a small mountain town. Some mountain climbers point to a huge tidal wave in the distance. They tell me I'd better go home for protection. I wonder how much protection a small apartment could be against a tidal wave. The mountain climbers are wearing glasses like my mother's who told me gently when I was a child that in every childbirth the woman goes down into the "valley of death."

In the next scene I am cooped up in a small apartment with two friends, Millie and Marjorie, waiting for the wave to hit. I am the only one worried; they are not at all concerned. In real life Millie always has a cheerful manner, which sometimes seems false. Marjorie, on the other hand, is a woman with a rather flat affect who doesn't reveal her emotions. She has no relatives except her beloved daughter.

Later in my dream, I greet Millie at a meeting. She tells me her daughter has recently died, but she says she is doing "just fine." The two women remind me of myself lately. I've been staying on the surface of life, afraid to feel the awful truth: underneath the calm, I'm terrified for my daughter. No wonder I haven't written much in this journal the past few months.

Besides my mother's warning about the valley of death, I must confess another reason to be frightened. Several months ago, as part of a package deal on a boat trip, Janet and I went to a card reader, who prophesied that Janet would have a boy, with a difficult birth. Although belief in magic is infantile, and usually yields to analysis, somewhere in my unconscious a remnant of superstition remains.

The tidal wave of my dream must be the coming birth. The mountaineers probably appeared as a result of an article I read yesterday about the difference between U.S. and European climbers. In Europe, when a climber dies on the mountain, survivors leave the body there to freeze, thinking it too risky to carry the corpse back down. In the United States, on the other hand, climbers will risk their lives to bring back the body of a comrade. In my dream, I relate to the mountain climbers, wondering what would become of me if anything happened to Janet. Would I be frozen forever, like Marjorie, or would I make it down the mountain like Millie?

To me, the significance of this dream is that no matter how frightening a thought is, you can't say "I won't even think about it." The ostrich with its head in the sand is a likely candidate for attack from the rear. It is better to face one's fears, no matter how terrifying, and use all one's intelligence to conquer them. Repression is a failure. The unconscious will out, one way or another.

Which reminds me that on August 11, I noted that Janet was having nightmares. Yesterday, I wrote that in contrast to Sam and me, she is now sleeping fine. She has faced her fears and put them to rest. Perhaps by acknowledging my fears in this dream, I will move forward, too.

♣

November 7

WENDY HAS HAD her anxiety dream now. In it, her younger brother, Eric, had to go down a long, dark tunnel, and she was scared he would suffocate. She asked me what it meant. I told her I thought it was a birth dream, and that her pregnancy brought back fears she had as a little girl, when she was told that a baby was in her mommy's tummy.

"You were scared the baby would suffocate in that little closed-in space," I said.

Wendy was relieved. "I was afraid it was a premonition about the baby," she said.

Later she said she had told her friends about the

dream and that all were relieved by my explanation. Accurate or not, an analyst for a mother-in-law sometimes comes in handy.

♣

November 8

IT IS NOVEMBER eighth, and Janet hasn't delivered yet. She was due on the third. I am like a runner at the starting line, and the gun doesn't go off. I'm too old to have to run for a plane at any unplanned moment. Worse, all my patients have been alerted that I may be called away suddenly, but don't know exactly when. So they are acting up, too. The absence of an analyst is always difficult for patients, but when they don't know when the leave-taking will occur, it's even more traumatic. Zane told Janet I'm so irritable he doesn't want to be near me. I know what he means. I'm like the car alarm that is screeching away outside my window on 87th Street.

Even my easy-going daughter, who had worked through her fears, I thought, is getting apprehensive. She told me yesterday that neither she nor Sam had slept the night before. She said she was afraid the birth would be difficult. I calmed her by mentioning a patient who had just given birth to her first child at age 40 and whose labor had lasted only two hours. I didn't tell her that the average labor in a first pregnancy lasts 10 to 12 hours.

Janet said, "You're the only one who tells me good things! Everybody else tells me horror stories. A woman from my Lamaze class told me a really horrendous one. She was a few weeks late and they had to induce labor. She

On Becoming a Grandparent

94

was in labor for a long time, because the cord was wrapped around the baby's neck. Finally they did a Caesarean. And the most awful part is that the baby's face was close to the mother's stomach, and when the doctor cut into her, he cut the baby's face. When I asked the woman who her doctor was, she answered, 'Dr. X!' And would you believe it, Dr. X is *my* obstetrician?"

I didn't know whether to laugh or cry. What kind of sadist tells a woman about to give birth about a horrendous delivery presided over by her own physician? The woman apparently hadn't gotten over her own traumatic delivery yet, and was working out her unresolved terrors on Janet.

And yet Janet believes in me. It helps her that I think the labor will go well. She said, "You're always right. How do you know these things? You told me a long time ago that the baby would be late. How did you know?"

I said, "You didn't look that pregnant to me. Sometimes you have to trust your instincts." Now if only I'd cope as well with my own anxieties . . .

♣

November 9

"MOM," THE PHONE RANG at 6 A.M., "did I wake you?"

"No," I lied. "Are you in labor?"

"Well," she answered. "I don't know whether I am or not. I have had these mild cramps on and off all night, but they're not regular. Do you think I am?"

"It sounds like you might be. If not, I'd guess it'll be in a day or two."

The Long Wait

"Well, I'm going to see the doctor at 9. Shall I call you if I'm in labor even if you're with a patient?"

"Of course."

"What time are the flights?"

"There are eight of them." I give her the times, one of which is 12 o'clock.

"Well," she said, "If I'm in labor take that one. But sometimes the doctor will say go home and come back in two weeks. I don't want you to come down here for nothing." Despite her thoughtfulness, she sounded as if she wanted me with her, no matter what.

"Okay, dear, we'll see," I said. "Good luck!"

I drag out my old *Merck Manual* and turn to "Management of Normal Labor," where I find: "The patient in labor has contractions that increase in duration, intensity and frequency. The rhythmic contractions are usually preceded by a latent phase, with irregular contractions of varying intensity that apparently ripen or soften the cervix. The latent phase may be intermittent over several days or may last for only a few hours." So her pregnancy is perfectly normal. I am reassured. I call Janet again and read her the passage. She is not comforted.

A half-hour later, I call again. "Jan?"

"Yes?"

"I made a reservation for 12 o'clock." She laughs. "What's funny?"

"I made one for you at 12, too. Just in case."

"Okay," I say. "I'll do my breathing exercises."

We both laugh. "Don't call me, I'll call you," she adds, "Sam's parents are already here."

♣

November 9, (later)

AFTER FORCING MYSELF to concentrate on three patients, I finally heard from Janet.

"Well, I'm not in labor," she announced with authority. "The doctor said my cervix has softened slightly. In a few days, maybe, but not today. And if the baby doesn't come first, he'll induce labor next Tuesday, two weeks beyond the due date."

"Are you upset?"

"A little," she answers. "But I'd rather have the baby come when it's ready."

I don't know about her, but I am relieved. Now I can make a few tentative plans. If she doesn't go into labor in the next few days, I'll go down on Friday and wait for the delivery. I can finish my working day and tell my patients I won't be here next Monday. At least I can leave the telephone and go about my business. I could, but somehow I don't . . .

♣

November 10

I KNOW IT'S RIDICULOUS. Janet's only one week late. But I'm terrified the cord is wrapped around the baby's neck, as it was around Zane's, and that's why delivery is late. Never have I wished so hard that I believed in an organized religion. Right now I could really pray.

I divert myself with thoughts of Zane, thinking that

The Long Wait

97

in some ways the new baby could do a lot worse than take after its uncle. Of my three children, he is the most like his father. As Rudy did, Zane appears larger than life. From birth on, he has had a much harder time than his brother and sister, but life has both toughened and deepened him. He is hewn of rougher stone than the rest of us. It is characteristic of Zane that when I told him I had described him in this book as granite, he laughed and said, "Granite with lots of chips and corrosions in it!"

When Rudy died while starring in *The Babe* in Denver, it was Zane who went to identify his father's body. It was Zane who arranged for the cremation, and for the memorial service held for Rudy at the Actors' Studio West. It was Zane who spoke at the memorial with devotion and humor, ending his oration with a joke, that "Rudy died the day before the rent was due."

He has learned the hard way what is important to him. In addition to his electronics business, Zane is an art restorer and a poet, whose works have appeared in anthologies of the American Poetry Association. He is presently writing a manual called *The Manic-Depressive Survival Guide.*

Zane has a bipolar disorder (which psychiatrists now consider a chemical imbalance stemming from a genetic disorder) and the emotional problems that accompany it. Understandably, he has been preoccupied with his health for much of his life. Unlike his brother, Zane wants to live a simple life. As a result of his illness, he has developed a wisdom and maturity far beyond his years.

Zane has had a terrible struggle to regain his mental health, but his determination and sound judgment have helped him stay well for more than ten years. Zane's strength of character would be a wonderful model for his soon-to-be-born niece or nephew.

♣

November 12

I'M ANNOYED AT JANET. Wendy said Janet told her, "My mother is driving me crazy with her calls!" And I phoned purely to comfort her because she sounded worried and depressed! So, I haven't spoken to her since Monday. I'm going to Florida tomorrow, anyway. If they don't want me, I'll stay in a motel.

I was thinking in the shower, "I don't really mind being angry at Janet, because it'll go away when the baby comes." Here is my old thought dressed up in new clothes, that a baby will bring about a rapprochement between mother and grandmother.

A patient told me a story yesterday that confirmed this idea. She has never liked her mother, whom she considers controlling and opinionated. She related that the one time she and her mother got along was when her daughter was little, when mother and grandmother felt close to each other in their shared love and admiration. Now that "baby" is grown up, the patient and her mother are estranged once more.

So I have another reason for wanting the baby to hurry up and be born. I want us all to be loving and close again. Since Janet became pregnant, our family seems to have gone through many phases. I wonder what will come next?

✤

November 12 (later)

THE DAY ZANE WAS BORN, on February 5, 1951, Rudy was on the road in Pittsburgh with Olivia de Havilland's *Romeo and Juliet.* He had a clause in his contract stating that he was to be given time off to visit me when I gave birth. But there was a terrible snowstorm that day, and even worse, the passenger railroads were on strike. Rudy had to travel all night on open freight cars to get to New York. My mother was drafted to stay with me to wait for the birth. When labor began she accompanied me to the hospital, and sat up all night in the reception room waiting for me to deliver. Rudy arrived 24 hours after he left Pittsburgh, covered with soot. Ten minutes after his arrival, the doctor burst into the waiting room with a hearty, "Congratulations, it's a boy!" and ushered Rudy up to see me, leaving my mother to burst into frustrated tears.

That's how I feel now, ignored. I had a dream that expressed this feeling. In it, Janet and I are to take a subway, a resemblance to the train Rudy boarded to get to Zane's delivery. Janet goes a little ahead of me and gets in the car. But the doors close on her and the train leaves without me. I am left alone on the platform, desolate.

That actually happened to my mother once. She brought my little brother to New York when he was three, and after taking him to Radio City, went to get on the subway. My brother, the first Zane, walked ahead of her onto the train. To her shock, the subway doors closed behind him and carried my brother away. My mother was hysterical, but some sensible passenger took my brother off at the next stop where my mother, following on the next train, was able to claim him. Perhaps the message in my dream is that I, too, will reclaim my child. But as it was for my mother in the hospital and in the subway, the waiting is difficult.

♣

November 13

WELL, HERE I AM in Florida, on Friday the thirteenth. (Good thing I'm not superstitious.) I couldn't stand waiting any longer, so I flew down where I could see for myself what was happening.

Nothing is happening. Janet is radiant, but I took one look at her and slowly shook my head. She just doesn't seem ready to deliver; she looks as if she's at the beginning of the ninth month, maybe, but no more.

According to her doctor, she and the baby are just fine. He said he positively would not do a c-section on a healthy mother and child. Apparently he miscalculated the due date because Janet neglected to tell him that she has a longer menstrual cycle than most women. So she may not be as overdue as we thought.

The doctor is planning to hospitalize her on Thursday and will try to induce labor with an injection of Pitocin, a drug often used for that purpose. If the baby isn't ready, the shot won't work, and he will send her home. Both Janet and Sam feel it would be better to "let the baby decide." We decided it would be simpler if I went home in a day or so, and Sam will call me on Thursday as soon as he knows if she's in labor. If she is, I'll come down

The Long Wait

immediately. So I'll have to be ready again to leave New York for Florida at a moment's notice.

I notice Janet is getting weary. She is tired of the constant calls asking, "Anything new?" A pregnant patient of mine was smarter and more self-protective. She told everyone she was due three weeks after her given delivery date so no one would bother her.

Janet wistfully says: "It's not fair. Everybody else is pregnant nine months; I have to put in ten! Almost my whole Lamaze class was due Thanksgiving, and half of them have delivered already. I was supposed to be next, and I'll probably be the last one."

Sam and I also had our first fight today, because we were both so jittery. It was about Christmas. Sam is the child of Holocaust victims who were orphaned at ages six and nine and forced to bring themselves up on the streets of Poland. As with his parents, the continuation of the Jewish religion is vital to Sam. He feels the celebration of Christmas a threat to his Jewish identity.

On the other hand I, an American-born Jewish child, was relatively unaware of the horrors of Hitler's Germany. No members of our family had died in the Holocaust. It was something that happened only far away from us on the newsreel, *The Eyes and Ears of the World.*

My parents were mildly religious people who did not celebrate Christmas, but in the non-Jewish neighborhood where we lived, it was the event of the year. I didn't understand that our neighbors were celebrating the birth of Christ. I only remember feeling very left out on Christmas morning when my Gentile friends showed off their new dolls and bicycles.

So when I had children, they got Christmas presents, too. They understood that for us it was no more a religious holiday than Halloween, just a time of universal goodwill.

Each Christmas that Janet and Sam have been together, she has come to New York for the celebration, bringing back Hanukkah gifts wrapped in blue and white paper for her husband. This year, because she was about to give birth, I volunteered to have an early celebration for my other children and to come to Florida on Christmas day with Janet and Sam's presents.

At this point Sam got furious. He yelled that he would not have a Christmas celebration in his house ever, and that he was horrified at the very idea. Even worse, he said that he would not ever let any child of his come to my house for Christmas in the future. He accused me of being confused about religion and of confusing my daughter as well. Then he said that if I had any understanding of him at all, I would never have suggested celebrating Christmas at his house.

He was right, although mine was an innocent-enough remark designed to please Janet. I really hadn't given a thought to Sam's feelings. I understand now that my family's ignorance of the 6 million deaths was not much different from the thinking of "the good people of Germany." I had denied the horror for a long time, but Sam has forced me finally to look and understand.

After Sam's blowup, he came to my room that night to ask my forgiveness, saying that he was under a terrible strain because of the baby, and the pressing responsibilities of his new building business. Understandable.

We all are under a lot of stress. I forgave him, of course. We kissed and made up. Nevertheless, the underlying problem seems irreconcilable. I'll make no more "suggestions" about what Janet should do for Christmas, but I suspect that for both Sam and me, to forgive is not to forget . . .

♣

November 14

AFTER 15 OR 20 years of normal blood pressure readings, since I began an exercise and diet program, my pressure has shot up to $^{150}/_{74}$! Janet said, "Put that in your diary. We'll take your pressure again after the baby is born, and it will probably be down to $^{100}/_{60}$."

♣

November 15

THE MOST EXACTING part of all this is dealing with my patients. It was stupid to tell them I'd be called away suddenly but didn't know exactly when. Of course, they all figured out why. Trying to protect them from a sudden leave-taking, I have made things problematic for them. Every day, each patient wants to know what is happening, and because they know about the situation, I feel they are entitled to hear the latest news. Not a good idea for an analyst with supposed neutrality. They all watch my anxiety level and are worried that I am not "with" them. That makes me even more anxious. Of course, the situation has brought out lots of good material about the births of their

On Becoming a Grandparent
104

baby brothers or sisters or their own children. In analysis, fortunately, everything is grist for the mill.

♣

THIS WAITING for the baby while everything else is on hold has occurred twice before in my life. During World War II when I was 19 years old and on vacation between my second and third year of college, my sister Pauline, married to a Marine warrant officer stationed at Parris Island, South Carolina, was pregnant. Since her husband was away all day, I was elected to stay with her in case she suddenly went into labor.

Days passed and no baby. On the Fourth of July, we went to the movies to see a Laurel and Hardy film, and laughed so hard that Pauline's water bag ruptured right there in the movie. This produced her own private fireworks, as Susan Ellen was born that evening.

I told Janet about that. We went immediately to the movies to see *Hello Again,* which was billed as "funny, fabulous and full of surprises." It was no Laurel and Hardy.

Then there was my first pregnancy, with Zane. I was three weeks late. Rudy was on the road and my mother came to stay with me. During those dreary, dragging weeks, everything she did or said irritated me. I must have been impossible to live with.

In any case, I wanted the baby *right then,* so I decided to do some exercises to see if I could rush Mother Nature. I kicked and squatted and danced the hora. My water bag broke. Zane arrived early the next morning.

The Long Wait

I told Janet about that incident. She kicked and squatted and danced the hora. Then she walked 12 miles for good measure. I am sure the exercise was good for her. But it certainly didn't produce any baby.

In *Siddhartha,* by Hermann Hesse, Siddhartha says, "I can think, I can wait, I can fast. . . . Everyone can perform magic, everyone can reach his goal, if he can think, wait, and fast." I have no objection to thinking; one might say it is my occupation. I can even fast fairly complacently when the need arises. But I'll bet Siddhartha never waited for a baby!

Freud had a similar philosophy: "The man who knows how to wait doesn't have to compromise." Freud was probably right about "the man," but he forgot to mention the woman. Freud changed the face of psychology, but his theories about women have been debated loud and long. He thought of women as inferior copies of men and, a man of his times, he neglected to develop a psychology of female sexuality.

♣

November 17

TODAY WHILE SWIMMING in the pool at the Holiday Inn, I think how wonderful it feels to bend my body sharply and knife down through the water. I wonder if swerving and flexing through the amniotic fluid feels that good to the baby. Recent research suggests that a fetus at 26 weeks cleverly moves about in the womb propelled by its feet and legs. Employing an elegant longitudinal spiral roll, it twists its spine 180 degrees. The fetus extends and rotates its head and finally the spine and legs, using the long spinal reflexes.

The sensual feeling of the water against my skin is exquisite. It feels that way in the shower, too. I have always believed that these sensations are skin memories of the early pleasures experienced by the infant being bathed. Now I'm not so sure. I think now the original joy comes at an earlier time, when the skin of the fetus is gently caressed by amniotic fluid in motion. It seems likely that it must be our first erotic pleasure.

Of course, Janet's baby is now flush against the sides of her womb and has no room to extend and sweep, to lengthen and tauten, to savor being a body. These days he or she can only poke against the confines of that tight little house.

Janet was thinking about this today, too. She said, "When the baby gets very active now it's like in the Tom and Jerry cartoon when the cat tries to get out of a plastic bag. It goes wham, smack, jab! You can see the arms and legs punching from inside the bag." Was being trapped in the womb both the fear and the fantasy of the artist who created that cartoon?

As I dived under the water, I noted the blue of the sky shining through. The sunlight made patterns that were very different from those on the shady side of the pool. It was fun to note the muted colors as I mused about my coming grandchild. Does the embryo see light and pattern through Janet's skin and flesh? Some investigators believe it does. The heart rate may speed up and the fetus may turn its head away if a bright light is shone on the mother's abdomen. The fetus's visual system is quite advanced. A sudden onset of light will produce an eye-blink reflex, and light will cause changes in pupil size and heart and respiratory activity. According to Thomas Verny, newborns are constantly looking at things, even in the dark.

But perhaps the baby is getting bored by now with womb light, old scenery. After all, s/he has developed many new skills that will possibly motivate her to seek a more expansive home. Couldn't that first voyage be instigated by the desire to seek a new environment? According to Freud, we must go forward in order to go backward, before we can regain earlier pleasures in a more advanced form. If Janet's baby is losing the pleasure of its primeval home, s/he will have to move ahead to recapture in more mature form that first-known gratification.

♣

November 17 (later)

WAITING FOR MY GRANDCHILD to be born has forced me to reexamine what I formerly had considered a closed issue. I used to believe that antiabortionists were crackpots, reactionaries who were unthinkingly carrying out the teachings of a despotic church. I have always agreed with the feminist philosophy that a woman's body is her own. Since she carries the child and has the major burden of responsibility even in these days of expanded fatherhood, it should be she who decides if the child is to be born. Absolutely clear, right? Now, I'm not so sure.

Here I am having a deep relationship with an unborn child. Studying the research that shows embryos to be feeling, hearing, seeing, conscious, viable human beings has corroborated my changing attitude. This is not simply a thing, a "fetus," that we are talking about; what we have is a physically complete, living person who surely has the right to life, liberty, and the pursuit of happiness as much as we. I would have been absolutely devastated if my daughter had decided to abort my grandchild. Doesn't the child belong also to her father, to me, to the world?

I remember a movie I saw long ago that starred Judy Holliday and Jack Lemmon. For some reason the couple had not yet had children, although they had been married for some time. The would-be grandfather shouts at them, "Where are my grandchildren? They have as much right to be here as you do!" Interesting that I remember only these lines from the movie. Perhaps I had conflicting feelings even then about the rights of the unborn.

I was discussing this conflict with a friend recently. "What about the pregnancy of a woman whose life might be ruined by giving birth?" she asked. "How about the offspring of a rapist's attack, or of incest? Shouldn't they be aborted?"

We all know that raising a child in the best of circumstances is not easy. It would be a thousand times more difficult to grow up as a child conceived in rape or incest, and many such children are given up for adoption. But I have found through my practice that it is possible for the offspring of a rapist to develop normally, if he or she is raised in a loving, caring home. Theoretically even the child of incest can survive and flourish, as the old theory about the transmission of acquired characteristics has yielded to genetic research.

I can see aborting a pregnancy if the emotional or

physical life of the mother is in danger. Her life should have priority; she exists, while the child's future is only a possibility. But I don't believe the life of an unborn child should be destroyed frivolously, or for any but the most profound reasons. The older I get, the more precious life becomes. At age 64, I can truly say that nothing is more important to me than the lives I've helped create.

And yet, despite being swept up by feelings about my unborn grandchild, finally only one conclusion is possible for me. I am a professional whose task it is to encourage the independence of selfhood of all my patients. It is not my role, nor the government's, nor the church's, to dictate the future of the unborn. In the end, if we are to keep our freedom, the decision to bear a child can only be made by the adults involved.

❧

November 19

HOME AGAIN and back to work, concentrating some of the time. Finally Sam calls. Janet got the injection of Pitocin. She had a few measly contractions, and then they stopped. So she went home.

❧

November 20

MARY KINERK has caught what I call the Grandparent Syndrome, even though she is not a grandparent or even a parent. Mary lives next door to me, has become interested in the outcome of Janet's pregnancy, and says she thinks about the baby all the time. Furthermore, the pregnancy has made her review her own experiences, just as it has for me.

Today, she rang the doorbell to tell me, "I never had a grandchild, so I'm borrowing yours." Then she started telling me her memories, standing outside my door. "When my niece was born," she reminisced, "Mother would let her get away with anything. I remember when the baby tore all the flowers off the poinsettia plant and ate them. Mother said 'Isn't that cute?' She would have murdered any of her own kids who tried that!"

Mary and I are far from intimate, but the story of her life seems to be emerging around this "grandchild," just as mine has. She is reexperiencing sibling rivalry and memories of her mother as grandmother. If the growth urge in old age is stimulated enough, a person like Mary who hasn't a grandchild of her own will adopt the nearest one around.

♣

November 20 (later)

THE WOMEN HAVE all had nightmares; now Sam has called me with his. He and Janet are hiking up and down the green hills of California. (Hills in dreams usually represent breasts, or the curves of the female body. As I interpret this dream, Sam is referring to the pleasure of their sex life.) Janet is pregnant.

Sam continued, "As we hiked, we came across train tracks. Suddenly, there was a train coming. It was heading for Janet's body, but I grabbed her and flung her aside so

The Long Wait

that the train only grazed her legs. But they were terribly bruised and bleeding, and I was horrified."

According to Freudian psychoanalytic theory, little boys from the age of three to five normally suffer from castration anxiety. The child worries that because he wants to love his mother, his father will castrate him. The remnants of this terror remain with practically all men for life. Some manage to move ahead despite their fears, while others always fear being "cut down" by authority figures or fate. Sam's dream suggests that he is terrified that his child will be maimed or killed during the delivery, as punishment for his sexual "indiscretions." But he drags his pregnant wife to safety, making every possible effort to rescue Janet and the baby from the very real dangers of birth. Even if I am wrong in my analysis, I'm glad Sam will be present at the delivery.

♣

November 21

KNOWING THAT SAM will be with Janet at the birth brings back memories of Rudy, my husband, who died just as he was about to star in yet another play, fulfilling the prediction of Lee Strasberg, who once called him "the best actor in America." In our marriage, I got used to being alone for long periods when Rudy was on the road with a play or in Hollywood.

Somehow I managed without him, because I knew I couldn't have become an analyst without his support. He encouraged me early to get training and then to go for my Ph.D. When I began to practice and carry most of the family's financial load, he never withheld his appreciation. We both understood the precarious financial rewards of the acting profession.

And within the parameters of an actor's nomadic life, Rudy helped me become both a mother and a professional, stepping in to help with the children when he was able, more because he loved me, I think, than because he wanted children. I've always felt that ours was a marriage of helping each other grow, what today would be called "giving each other space." The day Rudy proposed, I thought, "This man will let me be." He was not the typical husband of 40 years ago. When a friend of mine wanted to return to teaching, *her* husband sneered, "You won't earn enough to pay for carfare and clothing." She didn't go on professionally. I did. Rudy never felt diminished by my success, nor did he ever stop encouraging me. His best friend said, "Alma wasn't the first liberated woman; Rudy was the first liberated man."

I still miss both his tenderness and his practical side. Once he said, "You can have everything I've got but my talent." It is sad that he will not be here to encourage and delight his grandchildren. Rudy Bond's "bad luck" was a legend in our family, but I think it is we survivors who are deprived without him.

VIII

Matinee Performance

SHE CALLED AT 5:40 this morning. "How are you, Mom?"

"You're in labor."

"Yes."

"In the hospital?"

"Yes."

"When?"

"Since 2 A.M. And it hurts!"

"Are you doing your breathing exercises?"

"Yes. They don't help".

"Well, try the Grantley Dick Reade exercises. Take a deep breath counting as long as you can breathe in, then slowly let it out with a hiss through your teeth. It worked with you kids; maybe it will with your baby, too."

"Okay. I'll try it next contraction."

"Good. I'll be down as soon as I can get there."

"Don't rush. I'm only two centimeters dilated. You'll probably get here before the baby does."

On Becoming a Grandparent

"I'll get there as soon as I can. I love you."

"I love you, too," Janet answered—something we don't often say to each other in my family.

♣

I AM ON THE AIRPLANE with nothing to do but worry. I was better off calling airlines, seeing patients, paying bills. Then I didn't have time to think. Now I can only brood. Has Janet delivered yet? Is she in pain? Was I mistaken to tell her that I've experienced worse pain in my lifetime than in childbirth? That my cousin Mollie said it wasn't as bad as a toothache? Perhaps the delivery wasn't so painful for me because I expected it to be worse. Or maybe she's in so much distress because I told her it's not so bad if you relax.

Is she all right? Mary Welsh, an actress I knew 37 years ago when she was an understudy for Kim Hunter in *A Streetcar Named Desire,* died in childbirth. I never got over the horror of a healthy young woman suddenly dying like that. Sam would raise the child, and do it well. I'd continue to see them both and . . . Hmmm . . . Oedipus again (the generations are reversed this time)—Mother dies and the child gets the husband . . . I think I'll get Janet some roses, if only to appease my guilt about these awful thoughts . . .

♣

2:30 P.M.

"PLEASE, PLEASE, let her be all right," I murmur like a small child. I really could use a compassionate God right now, but I've always felt it is immoral for an atheist to get religion in a foxhole. One is asking God to be a "foul-weather friend."

A fragment of a poem I wrote when I was 16 comes to mind. I was a teenager and very enamored of a brooding, Heathcliff type who sat next to me in English class. One day, well into the term, Heathcliff looked on me and smiled. Blissful, I wrote an adolescent poem beginning with:

> *Oh space, time, stars,*
> *And all the universe*
> *yet holds*
> *to pray to,*
> *Let me spill*
> *the bursting vessels of my heart . . .*

Once more I call on "Space, time, stars, and all the universe yet holds to pray to" to help my daughter safely deliver a healthy child.

♣

4:00 P.M.

I WALKED INTO the hospital not knowing whether Janet was still in labor or if the baby had been born. I managed to bypass the information desk and rushed up to the third floor where Janet had said she would be. I asked at the nurses' station for Janet's room, deliberately not asking about the baby. The nurse quietly answered, "Room 207." I dashed to the room. There Janet lay in bed. I looked for her belly. It was flat.

"You had the baby!"

"Yes."

"What is it?"

"A girl," she said proudly. "I always get what I want!"

There was no time for details, because there was a sudden flurry of excitement. The baby was being brought in. Northwest Regional Hospital has a new policy: grandparents are allowed to scrub up along with the father, put on hospital gowns, and hold the baby in the mother's room.

I held my first grandchild for more than an hour. She grasped my thumb and seemed to be trying to put her fist and my finger in her mouth at the same time, never quite making it. Her name is Rachel Alana, she has a valentine-shaped face, a head of dark hair, and midnight blue eyes. "She's beautiful!" I exclaimed.

"I think she's ugly," Janet said.

A discerning nurse came in. "Grandma's in love!" she said.

I took a few minutes to run out to a nearby bookstore. "Have you any songbooks for children?" I asked. "How old is the child?" the salesgirl inquired. "One hour," I answered. She burst out laughing.

♣

6 P.M.

BETWEEN FEEDINGS, Janet and Sam described Rachel's birth. They were truly heroic in the delivery room. I'll let them tell their story:

Janet: "At 1 o'clock yesterday afternoon I went to the

bathroom and discovered that I had lost the mucus plug, [often referred to as the 'show' or 'sign']. I was so excited because I thought this was it. So I called out to Sam, 'I lost the plug!' Then we both got excited and paged the doctor. But in the 15-minute interim it took him to call back, I looked up the meaning of losing the plug in my baby books. To my dismay I found that it could mean either the beginning of true labor or that labor could start in two weeks. The doctor called back and confirmed this, saying 'All you can do is wait.'

"So once again I was disappointed. But about 2 o'clock I started getting a different kind of contraction—more like menstrual cramps. They were irregular so I figured it was false labor again and tried not to get too hopeful. But I told Sam 'This time it may be it!' And would you believe he said, 'I've got to get the bills done' and sat there for an hour and finished them!

"After that I wanted to go for a walk, as we were told that walking speeds up the process of labor. So we went to the Arts and Crafts Fair, walking for about two and a half hours. During that time the contractions got stronger. I felt a sharp pain, and I stopped Sam and said 'This really hurts!' Later, a friend brought in some Italian food. But I thought if this is really it, I shouldn't be eating. So I ate only a few bites, even though I was hungry. Also I didn't want Patty to know that I was in labor, so I went into the bathroom during contractions and just told her I didn't feel well.

"Then at 9:30, the contractions started coming every 20 minutes, piercing knifelike pains. Sam went to sleep, saying 'I've got to get my sleep.' I let him, thinking that if the contractions got real bad I'd need him more then.

"At about 11 o'clock I tried to get some sleep myself. I found that I was able to doze off now and then but was awakened every 12 minutes or so by the contractions. I went out into the living room, and remembering from my Lamaze class that it helps to keep walking, paced in circles around the living room floor.

"Then the contractions started to get really painful, so I tried various positions to help me dissociate from the pain. I found that if I held on to the back of a chair and squatted, taking very deep breaths to raise my diaphragm, that position helped the most. I also lay down on the couch between contractions because I knew there would be a long day ahead. By 2 A.M. this morning, the situation was getting extremely difficult to deal with on my own. I felt I needed Sam's support, so I woke him up. His first response was, 'Let me sleep another hour.' I thought, 'Some Lamaze coach!' But then he became concerned during the next contraction, when he saw I definitely was not kidding around.

"We stayed home for about an hour more. Sam kind of slept between my contractions, but every time I had one he would wake up. At this point they were coming about every 8 to 10 minutes. Instead of a chair I held on to the bedpost and squatted. The question was whether to go to the hospital.

"Then at 3 A.M., something strange happened. The contractions started coming in a peculiar rhythm. One would come in 5 minutes and another 3 minutes later.

But the second contraction would be only half a contraction lasting maybe 5 seconds. We didn't know whether to count them as 5 minutes or 3 minutes apart. We were scared the baby might pop out during one of them. We remembered this had actually happened to a couple we know. That's when we developed a sense of urgency, and decided to go to the hospital.

"It was cool and silent, a beautiful breezy night. Not another soul was in sight. We both commented about how peaceful it was to be up in the middle of the night when everyone else was asleep. It reminded us of camping out under the stars in California. I had two contractions—one as we were walking to the car, and one as we were going into the emergency room of the hospital. Both times I squatted down holding onto the door handle of the car. I was glad it wasn't in the daytime; people would have thought I was nuts.

"This time we made sure we had all our bags and pillows with us, because the first time I went to the hospital for the oxytocin stress test during the false labor, we had forgotten them. I said, 'We have enough stuff here for a week's vacation.'

"We walked into the emergency room admissions area, where a little old lady asked us if this was it. I said 'I certainly hope so.' It was then about 3:30 A.M. We went upstairs to the labor and delivery wing, which we supposedly knew the location of, having visited there many times. Actually we kind of got lost and ended up in pediatrics, because we took the wrong elevator. But a nurse who was standing in the hallway asked if she could help, and got us back on track.

"I wanted the nurse assigned to us to examine me so she could tell us if this was the real thing this time. So I changed into a hospital gown and was given labor room number three.

"A friend had raved about the nurses at this hospital. The one I had was aloof, however, and very offhand about the whole thing, which I certainly was not. Did you feel that way, Sam?"

Sam: "Well, that was the original impression. But as the morning wore on, I developed more confidence in her."

Janet: "I suppose I had mixed feelings about her diagnosis as well. She said the baby had not yet descended, which was not good. On the other hand she said that I was two centimeters dilated, and I was thrilled to hear that I was dilated at all. After all, for the past two months all I had heard was that my cervix was thick, with zero effacement."

Me: "What's effacement?"

Janet: "The cervix thins out and shortens as labor approaches . . . and zero dilation! But after going through all that pain, I had hoped the nurse would tell me that I was nine centimeters dilated and ready to push out the baby. Instead she informed me that some women walk around two centimeters dilated for two weeks before delivery.

"My blood pressure was higher than usual: $120/70$ instead of $100/60$. And my pulse was fast: 96 instead of 60. It was scary. The nurse said that I probably wouldn't have the baby until the next night and was ready to send me home. Fortunately, she called to check with the doctor first. He said, 'Keep her there,' as they were planning to try to induce labor the next day if the baby had not yet arrived. It was maybe 3:45 by now, and the nurse suggested that we walk through the halls to speed up the process. So we did. For hours."

Sam: "The nurse had also given us instructions that Janet should come back to bed every half hour and get hooked up to the fetal monitor to check the baby's heart rate."

Janet: "On the third time around (about 4:30), Sam started complaining about how exhausted he was. We kept stopping in the waiting room and he would doze off on the sofa."

Sam: "I kept asking Janet to just give me ten minutes of sleep and I'd be fine!"

Janet: "I got mad that I was having the baby and he was the one who kept dozing off. So he asked if I would mind if he went across the street for some French toast and coffee, for he felt that would keep him awake. I didn't want him to leave me, but he asked the nurse if he could go. She said it was an excellent idea."

Sam: (apologetically) "I was anticipating being there the entire day and evening, so I knew I had to get something to eat and some coffee. Also, I had previously enjoyed the restaurant's pumpkin pie."

Janet: "When he came back he was a new man, wide awake and full of enthusiasm."

Sam: "Of course I had just drunk two cups of coffee, which I never touch, so I was *very* alert."

Janet: "We then resumed walking the halls, and after each contraction he made me try to do 20 deep kneebends. I never made it to 20. I kept imagining my cervix opening up during the contraction. I'm convinced the kneebends helped to open up my cervix, because they enlisted the aid of gravity.

"At around 6 o'clock I called you. Sam had called his parents from the restaurant to say I was in labor and that they should wait for news. We continued walking. While we were doing the rounds, I saw a poster that was very disheartening. It had circles depicting cervical dilation from two through ten centimeters. Two centimeters looked to me to be the size of a quarter. Ten centimeters is about the size of a large grapefruit, and that was what my poor quarter-size cervix had to look like before I could start pushing.

"At approximately 7:45 the doctor—my doctor— came in. I was thrilled to have him, because he is part of a group, and you never know for sure which doctor you will get for delivery. Before he examined me, he seemed concerned. His first remark was that the nurse had told him I was only a couple of centimeters dilated and that the baby had not dropped. Because I was so overdue, this was not a good sign. His mood was serious and not at all reassuring. He said, 'This doesn't look good. You are overdue. The baby is not descended.' Then he said he was going to do another examination. I knew by his voice that if the baby was still high, he would do a Caesarean.

"In a matter of seconds, on examination, he became exuberant, shouting, 'She's seven centimeters dilated and the baby's head is down! I'm breaking the water bag and putting in an internal monitor. This is great! I can tell my wife not to cancel dinner reservations!'

Matinee Performance

"So he broke the water bag and immediately the contractions became incredibly intense. At this point he stuck an internal monitor on the baby's head to monitor its heart rate.

"Now comes the awful part. The baby apparently didn't like having the internal monitor on its head and its heart rate dropped dramatically. It must have gone from the normal heart rate of about 135 down to 70, and it remained that way for several minutes. Rachel obviously was in distress. In another few minutes the doctor would have cut me open. In an attempt to counteract the pressure on the baby and to raise its heartbeat, he kept shouting orders for me to change position: 'Left side! Right side! Get on all fours!' At that point, unfortunately for me, I had a terribly intense contraction. I couldn't control it or myself. The doctor also was yelling at the team of nurses to set up an IV. They kept trying unsuccessfully to get my veins hooked up to it and kept sticking my arm all over with a needle because my veins are slippery and difficult to puncture. They attempted four different areas on both hands. [She shows me the four bruises.] It was a time of terrible tension and confusion, because the doctor couldn't do a Caesarean without an IV. The nurses were nervous, too, because the doctor kept screaming at them. At this point he shouted, 'Get her on oxygen!' This process took approximately five minutes. I couldn't take the stress any longer and started shaking.

"Did I tell you about Sam almost fainting? When the baby's heart rate went down to 80 and the doctor was yelling to the nurses to get the IV in, Sam couldn't handle it. He saw the blood spurting out of my hands and thought his baby was dying. But he could have collapsed on the floor and nobody would have noticed. So he put his head between his legs until he felt better. It was worse for him than for me."

Sam: "I doubt that! But when I saw her shaking, together with the nurses failing to get the IV started and blood spurting out of her hand . . ."

Janet: "Then, thank God, the baby's heart rate returned to normal."

Sam: "Do you know what helped the baby's heartbeat? I lifted up Janet's right leg, and immediately the baby's heart rate picked up. I figured the change in position might relieve the pressure."

Janet: "But with all the confusion and the unbearably intense contractions, I couldn't stop shaking from then until the end of delivery. I also remained on oxygen. I stayed on my left side from this time onward until close to the time the baby was born. I kept my eyes closed."

Me: "Why?"

Janet: "I probably was praying for it to be over! I remember adjusting the oxygen mask with my eyes closed. And I remember Sam's voice trying to calm me, saying soothing words like 'It's okay. You're doing great.' But at this point, it no longer helped. I went right on shaking."

Sam: "She was shaking in different parts of her body. I would touch the part that was shaking and it seemed to help. But then another part like an arm or a leg or her shoulders or head would start shaking. After what must have seemed like hours, she asked me why she couldn't stop shaking. I asked the nurse and she said that shaking is a normal part of the transition period. After one intense contraction, I ran out into the hallway and looked at the chart depicting the various stages of labor. It said that nausea, vomiting, and uncontrollable shaking are all symptoms of the normal transition stage. I was discouraged, because the chart said the transition stage could last anywhere from 15 to 90 minutes. Janet's lasted one-half to three-quarters of an hour.

Janet: "Now the good part is coming up. I remember that one contraction was so unbearably intense that the Lamaze came back to me. And I tried to switch the breathing pattern to the hee-hee-hoo pattern reserved for the most intense contractions. But it didn't work and I completely lost control. I don't remember what I did— Sam will have to tell you this part—I only remember that I got terribly upset."

Me: "What do you mean you lost control?"

Janet: "I just couldn't handle the pain. It was too overwhelming, and nothing was helping."

Sam: "She started to hyperventilate. I remember looking at the graph and seeing that this contraction was the strongest one yet. During transition, while standing at Janet's side, I was looking at the monitor that measures frequency and intensity of contractions. I remember thinking that she was in much greater pain than before and that the contractions were getting closer together and more intense. Nevertheless during the transition phase, I had enough cool to discuss with the doctor such mundane issues as camping trips and his new home."

Janet: "I never heard any of that!"

Sam: "Also, during the contractions the baby's heart rate dropped to the 80s, which was normal. But as the transition phase continued, the rebounding heart rate after each contraction got stronger and stronger."

Janet: "Then the nurse asked, 'Do you feel the urge to push?' And I said, 'no.' I remember thinking, 'I wish I did because then it would be almost over.' The next thing I remember is that I did have an intense urge to push. I yelled out, 'I have to push! I have to push!' I guess the nurse told me not to, because the doctor was out of the room. So I attempted with Sam to do the breathing exercise that stops you from pushing. It was one of the most terrible feelings I've ever experienced. It was like having a horrible case of diarrhea and someone forcing you to hold it in."

Sam: "I kept saying, 'Don't push! Don't push! Do the breathing.' "

Janet: "He did it with me."

Sam: "We didn't know if your cervix was fully dilated or not, and if you had pushed you could have ruptured yourself."

Janet: "The next thing I remember was that the doctor still wasn't there, but the nurse told me to push with each contraction. I was relieved, because they had told me in class that it was a great relief with much less pain in the pushing stages. Little did I know that that was a bunch of crap! I was still on my left side in the labor room, and I remember the nurse holding my right leg up and yelling to push during each contraction. Sam was by me the whole time, trying to get me to push in the right manner, which I did with a great deal of difficulty. I was upset to be in the labor room still, and knew that I'd have to get to the delivery room before the birth would be over.

Matinee Performance

I remember pushing, and it was extremely frustrating because I got the impression from everyone that I wasn't doing it correctly."

Sam: "You weren't!"

Janet: "It was much more difficult than I had imagined. I remember I kept feeling that I had to have a bowel movement. But I didn't care; I just wanted the baby out. Between contractions I just had to lie there and wait for the next one to come. I remember yelling to Sam, 'It's coming! It's coming!' But he usually knew beforehand, because he was watching the contraction monitor and could tell when one was coming before I could.

"After what seemed like an eternity, I remember them giving Sam something and telling him to change into scrubs. But I don't remember being excited about it. I was too out of it."

Sam: "Before they wheeled her into the delivery room, the doctor said to me: 'You know, I was this close to giving her a Caesarean.' " (He demonstrates by motioning with his thumb and index finger a fraction of an inch apart.)

Janet: "I knew it! I knew it! I remember them wheeling me through the silent hallways, but I didn't see anything, because my eyes were shut. Then in the delivery room they made me push myself up and roll over to the delivery table. Then they strapped my legs into the stirrups."

Sam: "My first impression was, 'What an eerie looking room.' I also remember grabbing the camera in the labor room and making sure I had it. I didn't know where to put it, because I was afraid it would get in the way of the doctor or nurses. So I finally just laid it on the table."

Janet: "Then came the agonizingly slow process of the final delivery. It's blurry now, but I remember instead of being on my side, I was happy I was able to push in a semiupright position, with my chin on my chest and my back hunched over."

Sam: "And the nurses had told her to grab her knees. A couple of times she was too weak to pull herself up to grab them so I lifted her up."

Janet: "I still didn't feel I was pushing right, and Sam kept telling me 'Use your abdominal muscles. Relax down there.' I was holding my breath and pushing with my face and shoulders and not using my abdomen. It felt like trying to blow up a balloon with a hole in it—and was just as frustrating, because I didn't think the baby was coming down."

Sam: "After six or seven pushes she was getting all these red spots from broken blood vessels on her face. But I thought I'd better not tell her this, because she would have stopped pushing to look in a mirror."

Janet: (ignoring that remark) "I might have imagined this, but I thought the doctor said that he didn't think I was pushing effectively and that they would have to use some instrument to pull the baby out. Sam told me later that the doctor had mentioned that he might have to use either a forceps or a vacuum extractor.

"The most helpful thing was when the doctor put his two fingers into the opening of the birth canal and said: 'Try to push my fingers out.' That was a big help, but he didn't keep it up. I kept asking Sam, 'Tell the doctor to

Matinee Performance

put his fingers there, because otherwise I can't do it right.' "

Sam: "I said, 'Doctor, put your fingers there. She does better when you do.' A couple of times I thought to myself that I should put on gloves and put my fingers there to help her. But I wanted to stay by her side."

Janet: "In Lamaze, they taught us to breath deeply and then to let the air out slowly while pushing. But the doctor and the nurses kept yelling at me to hold my breath and not let any air out while I pushed. I remember thinking that my face probably was getting purple. I was frustrated because they wouldn't let me try the technique I had practiced, and theirs wasn't working. They teach you one thing at Lamaze and then in labor the doctor tells you to do something else. Every time a tiny little bit of air escaped they would holler, 'Hold your breath and push!' "

Sam: "I remember in the delivery room Janet gave a big push, and I could feel the baby moving down the birth canal. I told her, 'Keep pushing—I can feel it moving down. Another five or six pushes and you'll have the baby.' "

Janet: "Another eternity passed, then the doctor shouted to Sam, 'Come look! You can see your baby's head.' And Sam hollered, 'It's got black hair!' "

Sam: "I said, 'I can't believe this. I was born with light hair and so was Janet. This must be the milkman's baby!' There was about one inch in diameter of dark hair on the top of its head. And then I knew that very soon we'd have this child".

Janet: "I expected the birth to be very exciting,

dramatic like in the movies. It wasn't, because I was too traumatized. I remember one of the worst feelings of the whole experience was between contractions. I assumed that the baby's head was going through my pelvis and the feeling of pressure that wouldn't go away between contractions was unbearable. I screamed, 'I can't take the pressure anymore.' And the doctor answered, 'If you give another couple of good pushes the baby will be out.' I remember saying, 'Shit, I can't.' "

Me: "I've never heard you use that language."

Janet: "Believe me, I did. and Sam kept saying 'You're doing great! It's almost out. You can do it!' "

Sam: "It was so frustrating because a couple of times during her pushes, the baby's head became visible. With the push you could see the top of its head. But after the contraction the head would disappear again."

Janet: "Then I remember the doctor saying, 'We're giving you an episiotomy. You are going to feel a shot.' But that was no pain at all after what I'd been through.

"Then I remember a feeling of the most intense pressure I'd ever felt, and I realized it was the baby's head coming through."

Sam: "When the doctor said, 'The head is coming out now,' I left Janet with the nurse to support her in the upright position and went to the other side where the doctor was and took a picture—only one, because I wanted to get back to Janet and help her push."

Janet: "And when the head was out, I thought, 'He's going to make me wait to push the rest out.' But it went very fast and he let me push it out, which felt wonderful. And I said, 'O God, thank you. It's over.'

Matinee Performance

131

"And then Sam said, 'It's a girl!' and I said 'Are you sure?' He said, 'Of course I'm sure!' I had wanted a girl so badly, and everyone else but me had been certain it would be a boy.

"After that I remember the doctor saying, 'I'm going to push on your stomach to get the placenta out.' He pressed so hard I screamed and tried to push his hands away. I said, 'I thought I was finished.' Things happened fairly quickly after that, and it wasn't painful anymore, just annoying. I said, 'How does the placenta look?' And he answered, 'Just great!' But I didn't think to ask to see it. I can't understand how some women are able to watch the final stages in the mirror. I couldn't. No way. I kept my eyes closed."

Sam: "I looked at the placenta. It was in a metal pan. I remember thinking, 'It's much bigger than I ever imagined. And all this was inside her!' "

Janet: "The last thing I remember is that it seemed like it took an eternity for them to sew up the episiotomy. While the doctor was sewing, Sam was taking pictures. And I kept saying, 'I can't believe it's a girl! Does she have all her fingers and toes? Is she healthy?' Then they wheeled me into the recovery room."

Me: "When did you first hold the baby?"

Janet: "I don't think I held her in the delivery room. I only remember it in the recovery room. And I also remember that I didn't feel too attached to her at that point. I remember thinking 'Oh no! After all this, I finally have the baby and I don't even love her! But while I was still in the stirrups in the delivery room, I took the doctor's hand

and kissed it. I said, 'Thank you, Doctor, thank you, God, for my beautiful baby.' "

Sam: "And he said, 'Janet, you did great!' and I shook his hand and said, 'I don't know how you do this for a living.' "

Rachel's wonderful birth makes me think about the contrast between childbirth today and the way it used to be. The differences are both physical and emotional, and, in my opinion, they reflect the innovations in childrearing found among certain classes in the United States today. While the process itself remains the same, of course, it seems to me that each of the generations in my lifetime has brought its own improvements to the experience. I was born at home, and my mother was treated as an invalid and was forced to remain in bed for a full month after. When my son Zane was born 28 years later, I stayed in the hospital eight days, and went about "business as usual" immediately after. By the time the twins arrived 7 years afterward, my hospital stay had dwindled to five days. Janet remained in the hospital only 48 hours, and I understand some women now return home a day after their delivery, with no problems.

Women today don't have to depend on their doctor to relieve the pain of labor to the extent they did when my mother had her children. Training in natural childbirth gives mothers a degree of control over their body. As long ago as Zane's birth, I was a pioneer in natural childbirth and continued my breathing exercises throughout the long delivery almost to the end. I didn't find it excessively painful. I remember thinking, "This isn't so bad. I wonder what would happen if I weren't doing the exercises." So I stopped. Suddenly the pain was excruciating, and I quickly resumed the breathing.

Preparing for the delivery by attending class and learning proper breathing techniques is psychologically useful, to remove that old sense of helplessness. As a result fear is lessened, tension at the actual birth is reduced, and a less painful delivery is likely. The unknown is always frightening; classes, reading, practicing the exercises, and bringing the prospective parents on a tour of the hospital to see the site of the birth now help to make the experience more understandable.

The shared birth experience also brings mother and father closer together, as the couple goes through an experience that was formerly the mother's only. According to the *Merck Manual*, the father's "moral support, encouragement, and expressions of affection decrease the need for analgesia and make the process of labor less frightening and unpleasant. . . . Sharing the stresses of labor, the sight of their own child and the sound of its crying constitute a dramatic episode that tends to create strong bonds between parents and with the child."

It seems to me that the most important results for the future of humanity, which may well alter the future of psychology, have grown out of the presence of the father in the delivery room. Years ago, when the baby was presented to the new father, it took a while for them to get to know each other. As a result, psychology abounds with theories stressing the symbiosis of mother and child, to the exclusion of the father. My father said he had no interest in my sister, his older daughter, until she was a few months old, when she followed him around the room with her eyes. In contrast, bonding of father and child can now take place soon after birth and does not have to wait for a relationship to develop. Sam adored his daughter from the moment he saw that minute amount of black hair appearing.

My father, whose job at my birth was to pace the floor and hand out cigars, contributed very little to the day-to-day raising of his children. This may well have helped bring about the formal, distant relationship we had. With my own children, I also was the primary parent. As I have said, Rudy helped with the children, but he was always helping *me* out, not sharing the responsibilities of a job that belonged to both of us. It is different with Janet and Sam, as it is with other couples I know who have had similar birth experiences. Sam's vital participation in the delivery room surely influences his role in the raising of their children. Instead of considering the children to be "mother's job," Janet and Sam have shared the work of childrearing since the day Rachel was born. Rachel is a fortunate child, who knows that from her birth on, she has been central in the lives of both parents.

CHAPTER

IX

Postpartum Depression

November 24

JANET IS ALIVE and well. The childbirth was successful and, to me, glorious. I should be the happiest woman alive.

I'm not. Tears wait constantly behind my eyes. Deep down are faint stirrings of disappointment. I pull myself away from the baby long enough to ask what's the matter. What could it be? Rachel reminds me of the old Lucky Strike slogan, "So round, so firm, so fully packed," all 7 pounds 11½ ounces of her. She is healthy and thriving. What more could a grandmother ask?

But . . . she seems . . . like a little stranger, not a part of my family. She doesn't resemble me in the least, but instead looks exactly like Sam's mother. Nor do I feel connected to her.

Postpartum depression, when the womb has emptied and the mother's body is in what is like a state of grief, is a well-known phenomenon. According to anthropologist Ashley Montague, 80 percent of mothers who give birth in American hospitals suffer from the "baby blues." Ranging from a mild "blue" feeling to deep depression and constant crying, postpartum depression usually occurs anytime from the first few days after birth to several months after. Where there was once a satisfying fullness, a tightness stretched over an ever-expanding universe of hopes and dreams, now there is emptiness. The pregnant woman feels a sense of unity with her unborn child. That sense of physical oneness with her baby ends abruptly with birth. Any loss must be grieved for, if the mourner is to move on to a new love. Thus, the "inside baby" must be mourned before the "outside baby" can be loved. The mother's nine-month job has abruptly ended. In addition, what is she to do with the hormones that have nurtured the fetus all those months? Her body is still ready to nurture, but the space is empty. She is left with the shock of going "cold turkey" from one physiological state to another. The little tenant has moved out of the apartment and not yet into the mother's heart.

According to psychoanalyst Kurt Eissler, puerperal (postdelivery) depressions may contain a deep biological factor along with the psychological, "arising from the self-evident truth that a woman has reached the maximum of her creative potential in the moment when she has given birth to a living child." The peak experience of my life was certainly the birth of my first baby.

Now after this new birth, I feel the loss again, as if I were indeed the mother. My internal child had nourished me these long months. Now she has abandoned me. I, too, am left barren, my fantasies of reexperiencing the maximum moment of my creativity, of reverting to the period of young motherhood, of regaining my youth—all are gone. And in its place remains an aging woman holding a little alien, a newcomer belonging to her parents, not to me. A miniscule stranger whose very being brings me that much closer to death.

Despite my insights, I'm concerned. I do and say the right things, but, like Janet, I don't yet love Rachel. It's all too much to take in. By going into a "deep freeze," I'm protecting myself from being overwhelmed. I also know it is nothing to worry about, that bit by bit the feelings will return. Nevertheless, the image of a small heart-shaped face feels fastened onto my eyes, as if projected on them by a machine. The impression remains for days.

All my life, when I have read a book, I've pictured the characters in it as vividly as if they were alive. Then I would see a movie of the book and find that the people in it looked completely different from what I had imagined. I feel deflated like that now. Rachel is a darling, but she's not the baby I've been waiting for impatiently all these months, the infant I pictured when swimming under the water at the Holiday Inn. All modern technology has succeeded in doing is giving us more material to force us to the wrong conclusions. I pictured Rachel as a little Bond, a duplicate of her mother at birth. Rachel doesn't look at all like Janet. She doesn't even have the flat-topped head her mother had, as I saw it in the sonogram.

Rachel will be a source of joy to us all, I'm sure. But

she's not *my* baby, and never will be. That baby lives only in this diary. I think I'll have to mourn my fantasy grandchild first. Then I'll be able to love Rachel for herself.

♣

November 25

I WOKE UP at 3 A.M. thinking, "What? Depressed because Rachel doesn't look the way you thought she would? Are you crazy? Have you forgotten you almost died a year and a half ago? You could have missed the entire experience."

On February 20, 1986, I had just returned from a trip to Hawaii where I presented a paper on Virginia Woolf to the American Institute of Medical Education. Logy with jet lag, I thought that if I ran around the Central Park reservoir, I might recover sooner.

After finishing the run, I was crossing the park transverse at 85th Street. According to a witness, I stopped, looked to the left and right, and almost reached the other side of the road when a taxi doing 40 miles an hour came bounding through the light and plowed into me. The driver didn't blow his horn or make any effort to slow down. I was hurled 10 feet in the air and smacked into a lamppost 20 feet ahead, where I lay on the ground with one shoulder and one leg twisted under me. I suffered a brain concussion, a shoulder broken in three places, a quadruple pelvic fracture, and numerous painful sprains and bruises. I was in intensive care for three or four days, and in the hospital for a month and a day.

Possibly because I was a runner and take calcium pills, my pelvis began to mend quickly, so that two weeks after the accident I could walk with a cane. But it took many months to get back to a semblance of normal activity, because it was much more difficult for my shoulder to heal. For months, I woke up every night sobbing with pain. It often required as many as four codeine tablets to get to sleep at all. Usually an excellent sleeper, I took almost a year to get through the night comfortably.

Even worse, I developed the beginning of a syndrome called sympathetic dystrophy, in which the hand, to lessen shoulder pain, freezes up into a clawlike position. I consider myself very lucky that good health, discipline, and hard work have brought my hand back to normal.

I was given physical therapy every day, and was faithful about doing the exercises, so the sympathetic dystrophy syndrome largely was kept at bay. But I had only limited hand motion for a long time, and had to relearn how to write and eat with my right hand. Because my parents had switched my handedness from left to right when I was a child, I am somewhat ambidextrous, and I managed to function in some measure with my left hand for four to five months.

My children were unbelievably caring. I was not prepared for their self-sacrifice and devotion. Janet, hysterical on first seeing me injured and in the hospital, took a leave of absence from graduate school and nursed me for three weeks. Sam came with her and stayed as long as he could. Both boys and their wives and my friends visited often, bringing food, gifts and good cheer.

Although practically everyone seemed genuinely relieved that I was recovering so beautifully, some people had a strange reaction. It was as though they refused to believe I had recovered, as though they remained stuck with the accident like a needle on a record. Even to the present day, there are some who question whether I have healed completely. I must admit to a twinge of annoyance at their persistence. Do they enjoy the idea of my being impaired? Or is the horror of a similar accident happening to themselves so great that they seek reassurance that it is possible to survive such a trauma? Perhaps it's like after a death, when we often experience a feeling of pleasure that we are not the deceased. Whatever the reasons, these individuals seemed to need to keep me damaged.

This situation contributed to a terrible depression, which has been revived by my feelings of the past few hours. Shakespeare speaks of new sorrows reviving memories of old ones, and making "old woes new." My postpartum depression threw me back into the despondency I experienced after the accident, when all joy had fled and life seemed an unbroken stretch of grayness: Would I ever again run through the park or commune with a patient at work? Would I ever know the joy of rocking a grandchild? What about the books I wanted to write? Was I doomed to spend the rest of my life in boredom and constant pain?

But little by little, despite the pain and depression, I began to find enrichment in the recovery period. The moments of despair gradually grew less severe and further apart. Besides my family and friends, I was fortunate enough to have a nurse and a physiotherapist whom I loved. The nurse would sit up with me during the nights I couldn't sleep and, over chocolate ice cream, we would talk about our lives. My physiotherapist was a young woman in training to be an analyst herself, and we spent the long painful hours in psychoanalytic discussion. It was good emotional therapy for me, as well as physical. She kept me in touch with my professional self and away from the danger of getting lost in the identity of the patient.

A month after being discharged from the hospital I went back to work part-time, and I resumed my practice on a limited scale a few months later. During the first few weeks of work, a nurse took me down to the office, brought my lunch at noon, and came for me when I was ready to leave.

The flashbacks took a while longer to get over. It was more than a year before they disappeared altogether. But they were important to my recovery. Rather than seeing them as nightmarish memories to be gotten rid of at any cost, I found they helped me reconstruct the events of the accident. Like a dream that is correctly understood, they were instrumental in overcoming the psychological effects of the trauma.

One night I woke up with the image in my mind of a long silver pole. The angle of vision was a peculiar one, with the post thick at the bottom and gradually narrowing as it approached the top. I realized later that it was as if I were looking up at it from the ground. I didn't recognize it, but I had a feeling it was connected to the accident. I returned to the scene where it had occurred. And sure enough, there was streetlight E8502, which indeed was a long silver pole with a light at the tip. The second shock of hitting the post after I had been thrown into the air must have returned me to a brief moment of consciousness as I lay twisted on the ground, looking up.

But the most frightening flashback of all occurred

soon after I saw the image of the pole. I dreamed of a pure white light at the end of a tunnel, which I believe was something I'd experienced at the scene of the accident. In many of the memories of people who have a near-death experience, a shining white light is prominent. I surely went down as close as anyone can to the valley of the shadow of death and returned.

It is miraculous that I survived, and even more so that I recovered with such minor impairments. Janet believes it was because I was in good physical condition. Sam attributes it to "clean living"—no drugs, no cigarettes, no alcohol (only chocolate, when I can't resist). I like to believe it is because I have achieved that state known as "well analyzed."

But the "explanation" I like best I find in a recurring dream. I see Rudy up in heaven looking down on the scene. As he sees the taxi approaching me, he realizes that, as a newcomer to Heaven, he does not have the power to stop the car in its tracks. So he positions me for the least possible damage. He knows that one of us must be around to greet our new babies.

My depression lifts. An atheist I may be, but I want to believe my life was spared to allow me to be with my grandchildren.

CHAPTER

X

Evening Performance

"MOM." JONNY JUST CALLED. "Guess what? Wendy's water bag just broke!"

"Wonderful! How is she?"

"Nervous. You better talk to her, Mom. Give her a short-term course of therapy. I'll put her on."

"Hi, Alma," Wendy says.

"How are you?"

"Nervous."

"What scares you the most?" I lamely ask.

"I'm scared of the labor, I'm scared I'll need a Caesarean, I'm scared I won't know how to raise a baby."

"You'll be just like your mother. You think she's a good mother, don't you?"

"Yes, I do. Thanks, Alma."

Wheew, I think, what terrible therapy, just when I needed to be at my best. Whereupon I put the dish towel in the refrigerator and the cordless phone on the stove.

I rush to cancel my patients and a dinner date. Then I sit and think. The hospital is in Summit, New Jersey. It seems unbearably distant, even though I am in New York City, only a few miles away. The only thing I want to do in the whole world is go there. I tell myself not to be ridiculous. The delivery might take 24 hours. I may have to sit in the waiting room overnight, as my mother did. Wendy and Jonny won't even know I am there. Nevertheless, nothing else will do. So I call Barbara Sacks, Wendy's mother.

She understands perfectly. Wendy's contractions are already three minutes apart. Perhaps I'm not so ridiculous after all. I'll take the 12:30 bus, and Barbara will pick me up.

There isn't anything else I can concentrate on now, so I might as well proceed with a scheduled haircut. And since I'm going to be a grandmother again, I think I'll splurge at Kenneth's.

Walking down the street, I imagine the scene after the birth of the baby. Barbara, Wendy's father, Marvin, and I rush into the hospital room where Wendy is holding the baby. I allow Barbara and Marvin to approach their grandchild first. The baby is a boy. I imagine him looking like the men in my family, his father's head on Zane's body. I interrupt my reverie as I observe that I have passed Kenneth's by.

I must be identifying with Wendy, for I pick out the robe at the hairdressers that looks like a hospital gown. The haircutter says that many women would pay a fortune to have curly hair like mine. It makes me feel great; I haven't been complemented like that since I found my first gray hair. After the cut, it is still too soon to go to the bus, so I enjoy the fresh air as I saunter down Fifth Avenue.

It is a beautiful day, sunny and cool, a harbinger of early spring. I see a penny lying in the street and walk on by. Through my mind goes the adage, "See a penny, pick it up. All the day you'll have good luck. See a penny, let it lay. You'll have bad luck all the day." I go back and pick up the penny. I am not superstitious! But just in case—I'll give the penny to Wendy.

I feel very different from when I was in a panic about Janet's delivery, having anxiety attacks on the plane to Florida. Today I am content. I love Wendy, too, although in a less intense sort of way than Janet. But Wendy was already one centimeter dilated three hours ago when her water broke. She's had a good start.

♣

March 11, (later)

BARBARA AND I arrived at the maternity floor after the usual doubts as to whether we were at the right hospital, and trips to various wrong wings. At 2 P.M. we were informed that Wendy had been taken to the delivery room.

Our first reaction was joy that all was going so fast for a first delivery. Although the doctor had said that Wendy might need a Caesarean delivery because the baby's head was probably too large for her small pelvis, it looked as if he would be proved wrong.

As time went by and one doctor or husband after another came out and congratulated the respective grandparents who were waiting, we became more and more apprehensive. Finally, we fell silent, our eyes glued to the door. Barbara, who was afraid to ask for information for fear of bad news, kept sending me in to the nurses' desk to check on Wendy's progress.

I asked a nurse if it were true that Wendy would need a c-section. She replied, "Oh no, she's delivering vaginally." I had never met the woman before, and later couldn't tell her apart from the rest, but I threw my arms around her at that moment. I had reassured Barbara, but I guess I really hadn't been all that sure myself. I rushed out to inform her: "Wendy won't need a Caesarean!"

This pacified us for a while, but soon Barbara requested that I inquire again. I held off as long as I could, and finally asked pitifully, "Anything new on the Bond baby?" Those wonderful nurses. Never seeming annoyed, each time they told me what they could, usually, "She's fully dilated and still pushing!" It was only later that Jonny told us that one nurse had said, "There are two crazy grandmothers out there walking the floor."

By 2:30, we really were concerned, as the last stage of labor usually is a short one and over in a half hour. By 2:45, we surrendered all pride and took to inquiring of everyone who came out of the delivery area, "Were you present at the Bond delivery?" No one was willing to admit it to the "two crazy grandmothers." Finally a doctor who had passed us earlier and was returning to the delivery area took pity on us and asked, "Are you still waiting? I'll go in and see what's going on." She came out again at 3 P.M. with the news that "All the babies who were supposed to be born have been."

Evening Performance

This was the low point of the afternoon. I couldn't figure out why, if the baby had arrived, nobody was telling us. Unfeelingly I said "Well, at least the *baby* is all right." Barbara turned white at my remark. She was looking to me for reassurance about Wendy, and for the first time, I was unable to provide any.

I don't know how we got through the next half hour. The crazy grandmothers slumped in the waiting room's hard seats like rejected refugees. Finally Barbara cried, "Isn't that Jonny?" In the past hour we had seen a hundred athletic young men in scrubs and masks who looked exactly like him at a distance. But this time it really was a beaming Jonny, in blue paper scrubs, who was coming toward us.

"It's a boy!" he proclaimed, looking two feet taller as he threw his arms around us both. "The nurses say he looks just like me. I held him and I rocked him. Wendy thinks I did very well with him." Pause. "I like him." Then with a devilish smile he added, "All the other babies look horrible. With the little cap they put on our baby, he looks ready to go for a drive in the country."

"How much does he weigh?"

"I don't know. He hasn't been weighed yet".

"What took so long?"

"In this hospital, they believe in letting the family be together for a while before letting anyone else know about it. So Wendy and I just stayed by ourselves, with me holding the baby."

I silently thought, "That's a lovely idea, but how stupid not to tell us about it."

Our conversation paused as two nurses approached

On Becoming a Grandparent

148

pushing a little carriage resembling the ones used in super-markets. In the carriage was the brand-new Alexander Richard Bond. The nurses stopped to let us look at the baby. He has a cherubic little face, a wonderful rosy color, and small, delicately formed features. He reminds me of an Italian cameo. To everyone's surprise, including his doctor, Alex is a little fellow, weighing in at six pounds two ounces. That explains why Wendy didn't need the Caesarean.

In a gentle, soothing voice, I started talking to the baby, telling him how delighted we were to have him. Alex's eyes stayed glued to mine. This neonate seemed to understand what I was saying and to like what he heard. Welcoming my grandson into the world was just fine with him.

An hour or so later, Wendy was wheeled out of the recovery room. She appeared exhausted, but with a look of profound satisfaction. Jonny seemed pleased with him-self, too, wearing a kind of "look what I've done" expres-sion. He reminded me of his father when Zane was born.

As her mother, father, and I crowded around Wendy, Barbara asked her about the delivery. Wendy said she awoke about 7:30, feeling so much water under her that the mattress was ruined. "I said to Jonny, 'Holy shit, my water bag broke! We're going to be parents within 24 hours.' " It is customary to begin labor with contractions every twenty minutes, but Wendy's had started every five minutes and almost immediately went down to three. The doctor sent them right to the hospital.

I remember that on the way to my mother's funeral, I

had been incredulous that traffic continued to flow. I couldn't understand how life could continue in its usual way for anyone, on such a portentous occasion. It was like that for Jonny and Wendy. "There seemed to be an hour between one blue sign with an H on it and the next one," Jonny said. "I thought, 'Here's my chance to cut through traffic and have a good excuse for the police if they stop us.' So I rode a lot of the trip on the shoulder of the road."

By the time they got to the hospital the contractions were two minutes apart. Wendy's doctor was nowhere to be seen. But he appeared in time to avert panic. He had delivered two other babies already that morning, and that's why he was late.

He gave Wendy the announcement, "You are one centimeter dilated. Your cervix has thinned out. Probably the baby can get through vaginally, but it will be very difficult and you might still be here at this time tomorrow. I'd like to give you Pitocin to relax you. It will time the contractions so they will be more even, but it will also make them more intense. And then, if you agree, I'd like to give you an epidural. You still will feel the contractions, but the pain will be diluted."

Wendy, who always has difficulty making decisions, asked, "What shall I do?" The doctor answered, "Trust me!" At that moment she had a particularly strong contraction, so she said, "Okay, okay." Then he gave her the injection of Pitocin.

"I only yelled at Jonny once," Wendy said. "He kept saying, 'Push, push!' I cried, 'Shut up! You don't know what pushing is all about!' Jonny has deep gashes on his hands where I held on and scratched him. Then the pains got to be unbearable.

"I thought 'Why do I need this? I don't want to be a martyr; I just want a healthy baby.' So I asked the doctor for the epidural and he gave me a shot. Almost at once it felt much better. Then Jonny and I were able to laugh with each other and even to watch a football game on TV. The doctor checked me out and said, 'It works every time. You are now ten centimeters dilated!' I went up nine centimeters in one hour.

"He said, 'I guess you can start to push.' I said, 'Okay, let's get on with it.' But even with the epidural, pushing was the hardest part of all. I guess the doctor wasn't satisfied, because he kept threatening me with forceps. But Jonny wouldn't allow it; he didn't think it was necessary. So the doctor conceded and said, 'Come on. Let's go to the delivery room and try to push him out.' "

The proud father then added, "He was all ready to use the forceps, but I said, 'Wendy can push harder, she doesn't need the forceps.' I told her to push and everything would be okay. And she did. And it was. That was my main contribution."

Wendy said, "He's right. They brought me into the delivery room and the doctor asked me to push. It was horrible, but I did and that was it!" Here she lapsed into exhausted silence. It was not the moment for me to look for psychological insights.

I like the practical, realistic manner with which Wendy handled Alex's birth. She never forgot the reason she was there. She did what she had to do. "This is what happened, and this is what we did about it." Later she said wisely, "Nothing is more important than giving birth to a child. It puts the rest of your life in perspective."

Wendy's and Jonny's experience was quite unlike Janet's and Sam's. Janet prepared for childbirth in a calm, scholarly fashion. Wendy approached her delivery in a more spontaneous manner. I would say that Rachel's birth was dramatic and heroic, while the delivery of Alex was accomplished with dignity and efficiency.

Alex's birth has given me a more fitting key to Wendy's character. I thought she was interested mainly in fashion and her husband's success. But now I see that just beneath her small size, insecurity, and indecisiveness is an earth goddess with a refreshing directness and honesty, with an explosive side to parallel her warmth. When she is angry, she lets everyone know it. She conceived on the first try. "It was easy," she said. Her pregnancy was without any serious problem. And she had a normal, relatively easy delivery. We need that kind of common sense in our family. Jonny needs Wendy in the same way I needed Rudy, to bring him down to earth.

At dinner, I asked Barbara if Wendy had always been a realist. "Oh yes," she answered, "she always was a levelheaded kid. And feisty, too."

What kind of mother will Wendy be, I wonder? Will she respond to her children impulsively, intuitively, or follow the dictates of the "authorities"? I hope the first, as styles in parenting change, and authorities periodically waver in their thinking. In my opinion, the only sure way for parents to do well by children is to follow their own instincts. I suspect that Wendy, because of her tendency toward indecision, will alternate between listening to her inner voice and turning to the experts.

I also wonder what kind of relationship we will have, now that Alex has appeared. Will we be closer, more intimate, in our shared love for Alex? Will Wendy want me to help with the baby, given our philosophic differences in child rearing? Will Janet and Wendy become closer as they share experiences? I can speculate on these matters, but must wait patiently to find the answers.

CHAPTER

XI

An Arrow into Eternity

March 15

I'M MUSING ABOUT ALEX, feeling what all grandparents must, at least at moments. I know he will not necessarily be raised the way I think is wisest, that even though I am a professional clinician it is unlikely that much, if any, use will be made of my years of experience and training.

For instance, there is a major difference of opinion on the baby's circumcision. The *New York Times* of March 12 carried an article stating that a way has been found to reduce the pain of circumcision in newborn males. According to a study quoted in the paper, "A local anaesthetic, lidocaine, provides a safe and effective way to reduce the distress of infant boys." Apparently results of the research indicate that infants given lidocaine cry much less, sleep better, and generally show less indication of suffering than babies circumcised in the traditional manner. But this relatively painless technique, which has been available for a decade, is rarely used, the *Times* continues, apparently because of an outmoded belief that infants do not feel pain. Then the paper states that using the drug "has been proven to be safe, and what will make it commonplace is for parents to demand that their doctors do it."

I showed the article to Wendy and Jonny, and asked them to request that lidocaine be used on little Alex at his bris. But apparently the ritual circumciser has never heard of lidocaine, or for reasons of his own has convinced the parents that infants feel no pain at circumcisions. It is hard for me to understand how these intelligent people, including my own son, can turn their backs on science.

As a psychoanalyst, I find constant confirmation among my patients that body memories live on as long as the body itself. Wilhelm Reich formed an entire school of psychoanalysis called character analysis founded on this principle. He believed, for example, that early oral traumas may result in a permanent tightening of the mouth or spasm of the throat and chest, and in a chronic tension in the musculature of the adult. Similarly, paroxysms of the anal sphincter may forever represent infantile fears concerning defecation. In addition, I see increasing evidence in my own practice that the castration complex can stealthily infiltrate every aspect of personality, with results that include distorted character traits, excessive fear of bodily harm, sexual inhibitions, curtailed ambition, and fear of competition. But what is most devastating to me is the thought of inflicting unnecessary pain on this helpless infant.

Zane, who has spent many difficult years in analysis, was only partly joking when he quipped, "It *still* hurts!" He spoke for me, too.

An Arrow into Eternity

It strikes me again that the only serious arguments I've had with my children's spouses have been over religious matters. The basis of the upheaval around Alex's circumcision is the conflict between science and orthodoxy. And the dispute with Sam over the celebration of Christmas at least in part pertains to the preservation of Judaism as he sees it. The only one of my children's spouses who hasn't objected to religious doctrine is Judy, and she's the only one who isn't Jewish! Judy is Catholic, but her loving nature allows each person the self-expression he or she requires.

Her feelings about religion remind me of Abou Ben Adhem, in the eponymous poem by Leigh Hunt. When Abou was omitted from an angel's list of "the names of those who love the Lord," he requested that his name be written as "one who loves his fellow man." The next night, "with a great awakening light," the angel reappeared and "showed the names whom love of God had blessed, And lo! Ben Adhem's name led all the rest!" Judy is a disciple of Ben Adhem.

As for my response to religious fervor, I will go with Moses in Psalms 90:12, "Teach us to number our days that we may apply our hearts unto wisdom." I must learn to face my own numbered days, to know what is most important, to be there for my children, to observe my grandchildren growing up, marrying, having children, developing careers. Will they be happily married, like their parents? Will any of them have twins? Will my great-grandchildren look like me? I don't want to close an engrossing book before the story has ended.

I AM LEARNING there is a far deeper motivation for my obsession with this diary than my stated purpose: to study familial conflicts while recording the biology of birth. And this came clear to me, as so many other problems have, in a dream.

It was my turn to dream about twins. During Janet and Wendy's pregnancies, first Sam, then Wendy, then Janet demonstrated an ambivalence about having children by twin-dreams.

My dream shows ambivalence as well, but not about having real children. I am caring for my small girls, when Rudy comes to tell me that one is terminally ill. I am incredulous, sputtering, "What, what?" just as I did when Wendy told me of her pregnancy. I ask if there isn't some treatment for the baby's illness, perhaps the amber-colored concoction I've been giving them, which resembles Aslavital, the supposed cure for aging developed by Ana Aslan in Romania. Rudy goes out the door, abruptly stating, "Horse piss."

I understand that I am still a bit jealous of all the attention given the two pregnant women, and wouldn't have minded being pregnant myself. But Rudy's direct honesty tells me I cannot escape the painful exigencies of life. In Janet's case and Wendy's, there *could* have been death or illness in childbirth. But with me, long barren, the meaning is different. The dying child in my dream represents my own wish for freedom now that my grandchildren are born—the need to lay claim once more to my life. But there is something more. One twin's death could refer to the end of this diary, of my burst of creativity that paralleled the two pregnancies, and of my attempt to have "brain children" to rival the actual births. I am putting the last of my energy into these final entries, keeping a living twin to remind me of the magic of the past nine months.

But as Rudy makes clear with his earthiness, I'm kidding myself. Raising children is the real thing. A diary is only an anemic substitute. And I am fearing my own death, my own "final chapter."

I think carefully about this new development and how to deal with it. When I became pregnant a few years after Zane's birth, my father went into a depression. He was convinced that the child I carried would bear his name. Since in the Jewish religion, a child can be named only for the deceased, he was certain that the birth of a new baby meant his own death. Surely it cannot be a coincidence that I miscarried that child. On a deeply unconscious level, I agreed with my father, and aborted the pregnancy as a gift of love to him.

Now I share my father's fear—this time for myself. Somewhere, in a primordial sense, I feel that Rachel and Alex are my replacements. Perhaps that is why I felt "disconnected" from Rachel after her birth. If I were not related to her, I wouldn't have to die.

But despite my protests, my rational mind tells me different. The baby who is going to die is me, if not now, then soon enough. All the scientific means of prolonging life, as Rudy abruptly puts it in my dream, are really nothing more than "horse piss."

Shakespeare said it more elegantly, if not as succinctly. "Life is but a passing shadow, a poor player who struts and frets his hour upon the stage and then is heard no more." There is nothing anyone or anything can do about it. Not doctors. Not diet. Not exercise. Not potions. Not lotions. Not creams. Not even creativity.

☙

June 20

I THINK I HAVE hit on a solution to my fears. As always, I take comfort from my mentors. Freud said we all have the unmistakable tendency to "shelve" death. "In the unconscious," he said, "every one of us is convinced of his own immortality." Nothing prepares us to believe in our own death, especially if one is in the best of health, as I am. Freud gave an amusing example of the typical attitude to death, in which a man says to his wife, "If one of us two dies, I shall move to Paris."

Freud surmised that we welcome illusions because they spare us emotional distress and enable us to enjoy our pursuits. Nevertheless, he taught us the emotional and physical costs of maintaining these illusions, and that the truest wisdom is in facing the intolerable. "If you want to endure life," he stressed, "prepare yourself for death."

I was close to death in my terrible accident, and yet permitted to live to be present at the gift of new life. It's as if I have been given more time to fully understand my mistakes and my denials. I denied my mother—uneducated, emotional, doing the best she could—the love she wanted. I denied Zane's chemical imbalance. Now, with

An Arrow into Eternity

the births of Rachel and Alex, I can reconcile myself to falling short of the ideal daughter, wife, and mother. I have even learned to forgive myself for being me.

Human beings live in terror of dying because we cannot tolerate the idea of time coming to an end. It is significant to me, as a kind of age-related consolation, that the process of grandparenting, in Kurt Eissler's words, turns the psychological focus on death into "the preservation of a flow of time towards the future." Alex and Rachel carry some of my genes. Down through the ages, a little piece of myself will appear and reappear. I am not disappearing from the face of the earth forever.

Freud said the ultimate aim of humankind is for each of us to die in our own fashion, in a manner of our own choosing. How do I want to die? I was with my mother at her final moment. Quietly, unobtrusively, she just wasn't there anymore. She departed as she had lived, with dignity.

It occurs to me that she has given me an unexpected gift, teaching me to depart from this world at least as gracefully as you tried to live in it. Not for me Dylan Thomas's "Rage, rage against the dying of the light." Finally, after decades of resentment, I see how much my mother and I are alike.

And as acceptance comes, the knowledge sustains me that instead of "going to Paris," each day I am permitted to memorize my children's faces and touch the hearts of my grandchildren. I can find solace in these arrows into the future. To be a grandparent is to pierce the bull's-eye of eternity.

EPILOGUE

December 31, 1993

I CAN NOW, with some assurance, look back at the period of the births of my first grandchildren and assess the differences between what I had hoped for as a grandmother and a human being with emotions and expectations, and what, as a professional, I have come to accept as reality. I hope other grandparents will be able to learn from my experiences.

Janet and Wendy, each in her own way sincere in her approach to motherhood, have turned out to be quite dissimilar kinds of mothers. Janet, a warm and gentle mother, to a great degree models her parenting methods on mine, but makes important adjustments where she wishes I had been different. She feels that because of my studies and my practice I was not home enough when she was small, and plans to wait until her children are well established in school before working full-time. She is now studying for her doctorate, but goes to classes mainly in the evening, when Rachel, six, and Mia, four, are in bed.

Sam is a true helpmate to Janet. Just as he participated in the birth of the children, he does his share of child care. Although Rudy "baby-sat" his children, and I could not have become an analyst without his emotional and physical support, I was in charge and he helped when I requested it. Sam is a partner in raising his children, and he takes on 50 percent of the responsibility for their upbringing. He is like his father-in-law, however, in being supportive of his wife's professional ambitions.

Wendy is also a generous and loving mother. There is no effort too great for her to make for her children if she feels they would benefit. She used to kid me about what she called the "Bond halo," when it came to my opinion of my children. Now we laugh together at her, because it seems she has extended that halo to include Alex and Matthew. But we have no difficulty with this, because of course I agree with her. Jonny is an affectionate father when he is at home, but he must work long hours at his ad agency. Because he has less time with Alex and Matthew, his style of fathering is more like that of his own father.

Janet is a "softer" mother than Wendy. She and Sam find it difficult to be strict. It took years before her children learned to sleep through the night. The little ones often roamed about the house until midnight, causing the parents to despair at their interrupted schedule and lack of rest, but not enough to change their philosophy of child management, which is that a small child must not be allowed to cry, but must be picked up and comforted immediately.

Wendy is a better disciplinarian. After a few months, she allowed her babies to cry themselves to sleep. They learned in a very short time that nobody would respond to their wails and soon were able to sleep through the night. It doesn't seem to have hurt them, and though the lesson was harsh, it is an example of the kind of discipline that I now believe benefits both parent and child. Wendy used to say, "If I had Janet's children, they'd soon be sleeping through the night!" I believe her. Also, social life is more important to Wendy than it is to Janet, and she makes more room for it in her life. She likes to lunch with her friends, play tennis, and serve on charitable committees. As a result, she has less free time to give to her children.

All is not perfect within the family. There is an intense rivalry between Wendy and Janet that has escalated over the years, despite their children or even perhaps because of them. The women see each other only during family occasions such as important birthdays and Christmas, when they make lukewarm attempts to behave civilly.

It seems to me that both are zealously guarding the oedipal position. Every little girl has fantasies of overthrowing her mother and "ruling the roost." She gives up the fantasy when she can decide, "All right, I'll submit to my mother's authority because I have to, but someday when I am big and she is small, I will be in command." When she finally achieves the longed-for position of wife and mother, she understandably is unwilling to give it up to another woman. There is room for only one queen. In our family, neither daughter nor daughter-in-law will bow to the other.

The situation is a loss for both women. Wendy has two sons and has always wanted a daughter. A devotee of fashion, she would like to buy beautiful clothes for Rachel and Mia. She wistfully says, "I really could love those little girls, if Janet would let me." Janet, of course, thinks that Wendy's sometimes sharp tongue makes a closer relationship impossible.

Janet's affection for her nephews has more than once taken an unusual turn. Once, she and I were baby-sitting while Wendy and Jonny attended a wedding. Baby Alex was very hungry, but wouldn't take the bottle Wendy had left for him. So Janet breast-fed him on one breast, while the other was given to her own baby, Rachel.

What helps me tolerate the inimical situation is that when the little cousins do see each other, separated as they are by 1,500 miles and family animosity, they play together amicably, run hand in hand, and in fact seem to love each other. That they pretty much ignore their respective aunts (except for Aunt Judy, who has no children and who, by gift of character, is an all-accepting, uncritical aunt) is unfortunate. I feel the children's joy in each other is a tribute to the parents, who have been careful not to turn the children against each other.

Janet and Wendy aren't the only ones experiencing a repetition of the oedipus complex. I understand how they feel. I was Jocasta for a while, but not anymore. Parents are central; grandparents are peripheral. The balance of power *has* shifted. When my children were growing up, family life often revolved around me. Partly because I was so busy, we ate when I scheduled meals; frequently we went to exhibitions, plays, or films that I wanted to see, when I had the time to see them; and we visited friends or relatives when they could be squeezed into my already overextended life. In the busy households of Janet and Jonny today, I have to work around the needs of my grandchildren and the active lives of their parents. If I want to be with them, I have to tag along as they go about their business. I rarely get to see a movie I want to see or shop in a special store when I am visiting them. I have to return to my home to be able to act on my own wishes. That is the way of life. The queen is dead; long live the queen.

I may have been dethroned, but there is still an important place for me in the life of the family. I see my role now as a grandmother keeping the family together despite dysfunctions, animosities, and a certain selfishness. I can't favor my daughter over my daughter-in-law, and I try to point out to both women how each contributes to the conflict between them, and that keeping the family together requires patience and understanding. Often it is necessary to submerge one's own interests for the greater good of the group. I understand that Janet and Wendy will never be friends. But it's important that they understand why. After that, there is no reason to force them to be together more than necessary.

What's more important to me than a close relationship between the mothers is that I have a continuous relationship with my grandchildren and earn their love and respect. I know of many situations in which families are torn, and the relationship between grandparents and grandchildren is severed. A former patient of mine is currently experiencing this tragic predicament. Grace is a college professor, a woman beloved by many friends. Her son and his wife were divorced, and the mother given custody of their five-year-old daughter. The former daughter-in-law refuses to allow my friend to see the little girl, thus depriving the child of a loving grandmother, as well as the grandmother her grandchild. Grace grieves deeply over this, and spends much time and money in legal battles, trying to win visitation rights. So far she has not been successful.

I will go to any lengths to avoid this kind of horror story in my family. It is extremely important to me to preserve the intergenerational bond. Grandparents have a special place in the lives of their grandchildren and have much to teach and give. I don't want my grandchildren to be deprived of the hand that reaches across the generations.

Fortunately, Wendy and Janet feel as I do, and despite their lack of rapport, make the minimal effort required to preserve the integrity of the family.

Early in this book, I worried about the "rich" in-laws, and that the children would love them more than they did me. That has ceased to be an anxiety. They are able to give more expensive presents, but I have my own ways of giving. And it seems my psychoanalytic experience has taught me a way of entering their world. There is room enough for all the grandparents in the children's hearts. I don't know whom they love more, if they do, and I don't ask. For children as well as adults, there never can be too much love.

As I was riding on a bus down Madison Avenue today, I saw a picture of a model in the window of a beauty salon. She was an older woman with silvery hair. All of a sudden I thought, "I'm going to let my hair go gray. I've been coloring it for 30 years and I'm getting tired. What is, is, and nothing I can do will change the fact. Anyway, she looks lovely; perhaps I can, too."

Am I giving myself permission to grow old by thinking of letting my hair go gray? I suppose so, for feelings of relief flooded over me.

These past few months have changed me a great deal. Coming to terms with death after the birth of my grandchildren has taught me what is really important. Until this past year, minor catastrophes would throw me into a funk. Today, stars and squares instead of words glared at me from my computer. And I walked all the way from 87th Street to the 42nd Street library for some necessary information, only to find the library closed. I accepted both inconveniences with equanimity.

I'm managing to work on this book with pencil and paper, and my publisher will have to wait for permission forms. And I feel fine. Only a few things matter to me now: my family, friends, patients, and books. And I'm compulsive only about the books.

My happiness continues. As I walk down the street, I feel a surge of well-being. I find myself singing an old tune,

Happy, happy me,
I was born in luxury,
For I've got a pocket full of dreams.

Even better now, many of my dreams are coming true. My children and I have come to an understanding of family dynamics. Zane is well and has a loving wife who understands him and allows him the space to live the life he wants. Janet came through a difficult first childbirth and has two children now. Jonny is professionally successful and also the father of two. I now have four grandchildren, to preserve my genes through the ages. I survived a terrible accident and was able to continue my practice and be with my grandchildren.

I remember that after Rachel was born Janet said, "Thank you, God, for my beautiful baby." Likewise, the thought comes to me for my beautiful life. To paraphrase Martin Luther, who said, "Even if I knew the world would end tomorrow, I would still plant my little apple tree today," I say, "McIntoshes, Goldens, Granny Smiths, I still have time to plant a whole orchard."

READING NOTES

CHAPTER II

1. Much of the empirical evidence given in this chapter is taken from Thomas R. Verny, ed., *Pre- and Peri-Natal Psychology* (New York: Human Sciences Press, 1987); see especially chap. 1, "Ontogenesis of the Faculty of Listening," by A. A. Tomatis, and chap. 4, "Consciousness at Birth," by David B. Chamberlain. Dr. Chamberlain examined more than 200 empirical studies to come to his conclusions on the physical sensitivity, initiative, emotional involvement, expression, and mental activity found in infants at birth. I owe these scientists a debt of gratitude.

2. Karen Horney, *Self Analysis* (New York: W. W. Norton, 1942).

3. R. M. Bradley and L. B. Stern, "The Development of the Human Taste Bud during the Foetal Period." *Journal of Anatomy* 101 (1967), 743–752.

4. J. E. Steiner, "Human Facial Expressions in Response to Taste and Smell Stimulation." *Advances in Child Development and Behavior* 13 (1979), 257–295.

5. H. Rottwarg, J. N. Muzio, and W. C. Dement, "Ontogenetic Development of the Human Sleep-Dream Cycle." *Science* 152 (1966), 604–619.

6.　Sigmund Freud 1920, *Beyond the Pleasure Principle*, *Standard Edition*, vol. 18 (1955, 38).

7.　Thomas Verny, *The Secret Life of the Unborn Child* (New York: Summit Books, 1981), 42.

8.　Lieberman, Michael, as quoted by L. W. Sontag, "Somatophysics of Personality and Body Function," in *Fetal Growth and Development* by Harry A. Weisman and George R. Kerr, New York: McGraw-Hill, 1970, 265.

9.　*The Merck Manual of Diagnosis and Therapy* (Rahway, N.J.: Merck Sharp & Dohme Research Laboratories, 1987), 1785.

10.　F. Roswell and G. Natchez, *Reading Disabilities*, 4th ed. (New York: Basic Books, 1989).

11.　Thiery et al., "Vaginitis uterinus." *Journal of Obstetrics and Gynaecology of the British Commonwealth* 80 (1973), 183–185.

12.　R. C. Goodlin, *Care of the Fetus* (New York: Harper, 1979).

13.　G. Klauser, "Die vorgeburtliche entstehung der sprache als anthropologisches problem: Der rhythmus als organisator der menschlichen entwicklung" (Stuttgart: Ferdinand Enke Verlag, 1971); as quoted in Verny, *Pre- and Peri-Natal Psychology*. A. F. Korner and E. B. Thoman, "The Relative Efficacy of Contact and Vestibular-Proprioceptive Stimulation in Soothing Neonates," *Child Development* 43 (1972), 443–453. A. Macfarlane, *The Psychology of Childbirth* (London: Fontana/Open Books, 1977), quotation.

14.　Henry Truby, as quoted in Verny, *The Secret Life of the Unborn Child*, 21.

15.　Michele Clements, "Observations of Certain Aspects of Neonatal Behavior in Response to Auditory Stimuli." Paper presented at the Fifth International Congress of Psychosomatic Obstetrics and Gynecology, Rome, 1977; as quoted in Verny, *The Secret Life of the Unborn Child*, 39.

CHAPTER III

1. A. Bond, D. Franco, and A. K. Richards, *Dream Portrait* (Madison, Conn.: International Universities Press, 1993).

2. Sigmund Freud, 1900, The Interpretation of Dreams, *Standard Edition,* vol. 5 (1953), 573–587.

CHAPTER IV

1. Sigmund Freud, 1921, Group Psychology and the Analysis of the Ego, *Standard Edition,* vol. 18 (1955), 107.

2. *Diagnostic and Statistical Manual of Mental Disorders,* Ed: Robert L. Spitzer (et al), 1980, American Psychiatric Association, 57–59.

3. Margaret S. Mahler, "On the Significance of the Normal Separation-Individuation Phase." In M. Schur, ed., *Drives, Affects, Behavior,* vol. 2 (New York: International Universities Press, 1965), 161–169.

4. A more detailed description of this case can be found in Alma Halbert Bond, "Sadomasochistic Patterns in an 18-month-old Child," *International Journal of Psycho-analysis* 48 (1967), Part 4.

5. Sigmund Freud, 1909, Analysis of a Phobia in a Five-Year-Old Boy, *Standard Edition,* vol. 10 (1955), 5–149.

6. Alma H. Bond, "The Split." Reprinted from *Voices* 11, no. 2, issue 40 (Summer 1975), 59.

7. A Meltzoff and M. K. Moore, "Imitation of Facial and Manual Gestures by Human Neonates." *Science* (July 1977), 75–78.

8. T. Field, "Newborns Mimic Happy, Sad, Surprised Faces." *Brain/Mind Bulletin* (Nov. 22, 1982).

CHAPTER V

1. George F. Salomon, "The Mind Connection," AARP Bulletin, Oct. 1993, vol. 34, No. 9, 2.

Notes

Chapter VI

1. Ernest Hartmann, *Self* Magazine, July, 1987, 97, quoted in "Dreams Don't Lie", by Diane Hales.

2. Diane Hales, "Dreams Don't Lie." *Self* Magazine, July, 1987, 96–97.

3. C. Trevarthen, "The Psychology of Speech Development." *Neuroscience Research Progress Bulletin*, 1974, 12 (4), 570–585.

Chapter VII

1. A. W. Liley, "The Foctus as a Personality," *Australian and New Zealand Journal of Psychiatry*, 1972, 6 (2), 99–105.

2. J. S. Werner and E. R. Siqueland. "Visual Recognition Memory in the Pre-term Infant." *Infant Behavior and Development*, 1978, 1, 79–94.

3. Thomas R. Verny, op. cit., 74.

Chapter IX

1. Ashley Montague, 21st Century Obstetrics Now! 1977. Marble Hill, MO:NAPSAC, Inc., 597.

2. Kurt Eissler, *The Psychiatrist and the Dying Patient,* 1955. New York: Internal Universities Press, 77.

Chapter XI

1. *New York Times,* March 12, 1988.

2. Sigmund Freud, 1915, Thoughts for the Times on War and Death, *Standard Edition,* vol. 14, (1957), 289–290, 298, 300.

3. Sigmund Freud, Beyond the Pleasure Principle, op. cit., 39.

6. Kurt Eissler, *The Psychiatrist and the Dying Patient,* op. cit., 292.

Notes

7.   Sigmund Freud, Beyond the Pleasure Principle, op. cit., 39.

EPILOGUE

1.   Wilhelm Reich, *Character Analysis* (New York: Orgone Institute Press, 1949).